Play guitar with Happy Traum.

Basic Guitar Lessons.

Omnibus Edition

Order No. AM 92880
US International Standard Book Number: 0.8256.1459.7
UK International Standard Book Number: 0.7119.4955.7

Exclusive Distributors:
Music Sales Corporation
257 Park Avenue South, New York, NY 10010 USA
Music Sales Limited
8/9 Frith Street, London W1V 5TZ England
Music Sales Pty. Limited
120 Rothschild Street, Rosebery, Sydney, NSW 2018, Australia

Printed in the United States of America by
Vicks Lithograph and Printing Corporation

D1404122

Amsco Publications
New York • London • Paris • New York

Book One

Getting Started 2
Holding the Guitar 2
  The Pick 3
Notes on the First String 3
  First Tunes on the First String 4
Notes on the Second String 6
Rhythm Session: Quarter Notes and Half Notes 6
Review: The Notes You've Learned So far 8
Rhythm Session: Whole Notes 10
Notes on the Third String 11
Review: The Notes You've Learned So Far 11
  Four Folk Songs on Three Strings 12
Music Basics 13
  Time 13
Rhythm Session: The Dotted Half Note 14
Combining Notes Into Chords 15
  The Tie 16
Review: Writing Your Own Song 18
Notes on the Fourth String 19
Rhythm Session: Eighth Notes 21
Techniques and Touches 21
  Alternating Pick Strokes 21
  The Pick-Up 22
Notes on the Fifth String 25
Music Basics 26
  Ledger Lines 26
  Rests 27
  The F Chord 29
  Playing the F Chord 29
Notes on the Sixth String 31
Review: The 17 Notes So Far 32
  Six String Exercise 32
Rhythm Session: Syncopation 34
Music Basics 37
  Chord Diagrams 37
  Sharps and Flats 38
Rhythm Session: Dotted Quarter Notes 40
Tuning Your Guitar 45
  Tuning Without a Piano or Pitchpipe 46
Glossary of Terms 47

Book Two

Notes for Review *2*
Songs for Review *3*
Chords for Review *5*
  Playing Rhythm Chords *6*
Playing Melody with Chord Accompaniment: Solo *7*
Playing Scales *9*
Playing in the Key of G *10*
  Playing with Chord Accompaniment in G *11*
Playing in the Key of F *13*
Playing High A *15*
Chord Review: Harmonizing a Song *16*
  Two Bluegrass Breakdowns *17*
  Some Musical Terms You Should Know *18*
Rhythm Session: 6/8 Time *19*
Work Sheet: Addition in 6/8 Time *20*
Playing Arpeggios *21*
Playing in Minor Keys *23*
Basic Chords in A Minor *25*
Chord Practice: Key of A Minor *28*
Basic Chords in E Minor *29*
Chord Practice: Key of E Minor *31*
Rhythm Session: Triplets *32*
Playing in the key of D *34*
Playing Chords in D *36*
  Bass-Chord Accompaniment Pattern in D *37*
Playing Rhythm Guitar *39*
Country Rhythm: The Bluegrass Strum *41*
  Playing the Calypso Rhythm *43*
Graduation Recital *44*
Chord Chart of Major, Dominant 7th, and Minor Chords *47*

Book Three

Review *2*
Playing Finger-Style Guitar *3*
  The Free Stroke *4*
  The Thumb *5*
  Right Hand Exercises *6*
The Bass-Chord Combination *7*
Playing Arpeggios *9*
  Using Arpeggios For Song Accompaniment *11*
Playing in the Key of D Minor *14*
  Basic Chords in D Minor *14*
Chord Progressions *16*
Solo Playing: Melody with Accompaniment *19*
  The Rest Stroke *19*
Review: Tempo Markings *21*

Playing the Melody on the High Strings *23*
  Playing notes in Harmony (6ths) *24*
  Playing the G Scale in 6ths *26*
  Treble Melody and Accompaniment *27*
Playing in the Key of A *29*
  Basic Chords in A *30*
Playing in the Key of E *33*
  Basic Chords in E *34*
Review *36*
Techniques and Touches: Hammers, Slides, and Pulls *37*
Rhythm Session: 12/8 Time *40*
Review *40*
Rhythm Session: Counting in 12/8 Time *41*
Playing Folk-Style Fingerpicking *43*
Graduation Recital *46*

Book Four

Review *2*
  Songs for Review *3*
Two Bluegrass Songs *5*
Rhythm Session: Sixteenth Notes *5*
  High B and C *7*
Intervals *9*
Work Sheet: Thirds *9*
Playing Harmonized Scales *10*
Work Sheet: Harmonizing Practice *11*
Harmonizing a melody *12*
  Harmonizing and Ear-Training *13*
Rhythm Session: Dotted Eighth Notes *14*
  Playing F, F Sharp, and G on the Second String *16*
  The G Scale in Thirds *18*
  The G Scale in Tenths *21*
Playing Folk-Style Picking Patterns *22*
Chord Building *27*
  Triads *27*
  Work Sheet *27*
  Sevenths *28*
Playing Movable Chords *29*
Playing Chords in the Key of B Minor *31*
Playing Diminished Sevenths *33*
Review *36*
  Playing Accidentals *36*
The Barre *39*
  The 3-String Barre: F Minor Position *39*
  Quiz *39*
  Combining Movable F and F Minor Chord Positions *40*
Chord Study: Other Useful Movable Positions *42*
Techniques and Touches: The Capo *43*
  Capo Quiz *43*
Graduation Recital *44*

Play guitar with Happy Traum.

Basic Guitar Lessons.

Book One.

This book has been carefully designed to teach elementary note-reading, music theory and guitar technique to the beginner. All the songs were chosen for programmed learning and take the place of formal exercises in order to retain interest and enjoyment.

Nevertheless, it is important that the teacher guide the student through this book, working with him or her and providing accompaniment on a second guitar whenever possible. (Several rounds and duets with chords provided above the melody lines have been written for that purpose.) In this way, the student will develop a sense of time and a feeling of playing with others. Most important he or she will establish the spirit of making music right from the start.

I have utilized a system of tablature in certain sections of the book in order to help the student past some traditional stumbling blocks. This tablature is written above the staff, and uses a large number (representing the string) and a smaller number next to it (representing the fret). Therefore, 2^1 means that the second string, first fret, or a c note, is played. This system gives the student an immediate visualization of where a particular note is played on the fingerboard. Through this reading-readiness approach he learns traditional note-reading. I have not notated the left hand fingering in most cases. In places where it is necessary, the teacher may write in appropriate fingering.

Naturally, each teacher has a preferred technique for guiding a student through the various aspects of guitar study. Knowing this, I have provided a basis by which the intelligent instructor can infuse this method with his or her own spirit and teaching style. All of the basics are here, yet the open feeling of the book invites the participation of the teacher.

Our mutual aim is to develop the student's musical potential and to instill a love of the instrument.

Happy Traum

Order No. AM 34901
International Standard Book Number: 0.8256.2356.1

Exclusive Distributors:
Music Sales Corporation
257 Park Avenue South, New York, NY 10010 USA
Music Sales Limited
8/9 Frith Street, London W1V 5TZ England
Music Sales Pty. Limited
120 Rothschild Street, Rosebery, Sydney, NSW 2018, Australia

The Author would like to thank Alan de Mause for his invaluable
contribution of ideas and material in the presentation of this book.

Printed in the United States of America by
Vicks Lithograph and Printing Corporation

Amsco Publications
London/New York/Sydney

Getting Started

Think of this book as your key to the world of the guitar. If you use it correctly, it will open many doors. It will teach you guitar techniques, develop your coordination and manual dexterity, and provide you with a basic understanding of music—in short, it will start you on the path toward becoming a well-rounded musician. Using this book should be an enjoyable experience, and will enable you to progress rapidly by playing a varied and interesting repertoire ranging from traditional folk songs to classical pieces, and even some country, blues and rock solos.

In order to get the maximum benefit from this book, the lessons must be studied in sequence (don't skip anything). Practice each section until you can play it smoothly and effortlessly. Each exercise and song has its place in your development, and it is very important to treat each one with equal emphasis.

Your teacher will provide you with the guidelines and pacing necessary to progress most effectively. With his or her guidance and this book, you will move quickly and easily on your way to becoming an accomplished guitarist.

Good luck!

Holding The Guitar

Sit comfortably with the guitar resting on your right leg. The neck of the guitar should extend to the left in a horizontal position. Try to hold the guitar in a secure but relaxed manner.

The guitar is strummed or picked with your right hand. Pick in a downward direction, unless otherwise indicated.

Your left hand presses the strings to the fingerboard to change the notes. Press firmly with the tips of your fingers, making certain not to touch the neighboring strings.

The Pick

The pick is held between the thumb and forefinger, but not gripped too tightly. To start, hold your right hand in a relaxed way so that your fingers are curled half-way between open and closed. Lay your thumb gently on the side of your index finger so that the outside edge of your first thumb-joint is about even with the first joint of your index finger. Your other three fingers should be relaxed, not clenched in a fist. Now slip the pick between your thumb and index finger with the point perpendicular to your index fingernail.

The pick should strike the strings as perpendicular as possible. Practice until you get a clear sharp tone with good control. Try to keep your wrist and arm relaxed, so you can attain a smooth motion.

Notes On The First String

Playing E

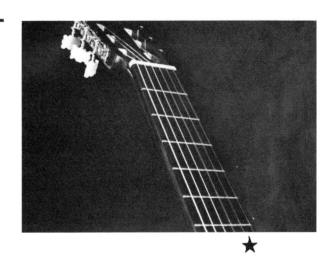

Play evenly. Pick downward on the open first string (1°):

Playing **F**

Press behind the first fret of the first string to play F (1¹). Use your first finger.

Play evenly, with equal time between the notes. Pick downward.

Playing **G**

Press behind the third fret of the first string to play G (1³). Use your third finger.

If the string makes a buzzing sound you are probably not pressing firmly enough right behind the fret. Keep trying until you get a nice clear note.

Play evenly.

First Tunes On The First String

Play slowly and evenly.

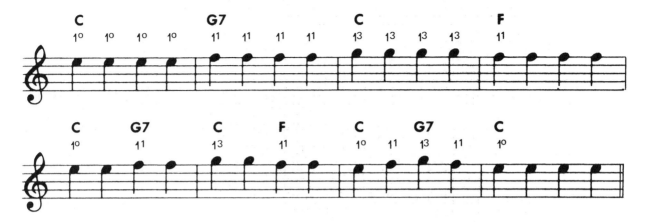

Now count out loud as you play.

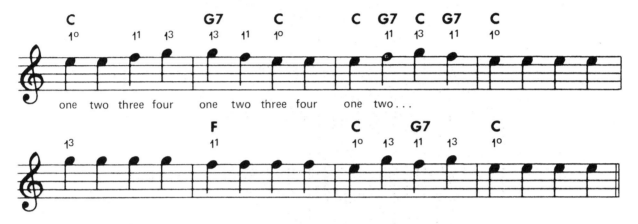

one two three four   one two three four   one two...

First Duet

student

teacher

student

teacher

Notes On The Second String

Playing B

Pick down on the open second string (2°).

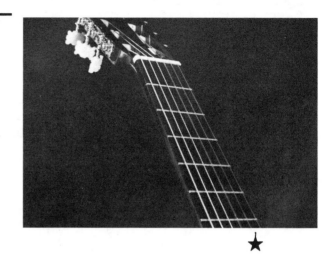

★

Count evenly.

| 2° | 2° | 2° | 2° |

one two three four   one two....

Count half notes and quarter notes carefully.

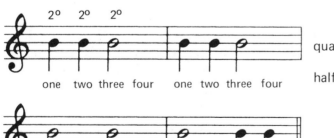

| 2° | 2° | 2° |

one two three four   one two three four

one two three four   one two three four

Rhythm Session:
Quarter Notes
And Half Notes

quarter note ♩ = 1 beat

half note 𝅗𝅥 = 2 beats

Playing **C**

Press behind the first fret of the second string to play C (2^1). Use your first finger. Be sure to hold the half notes for two full beats.

Playing **D**

Press behind the third fret of the second string to play D (2^3). Use your third finger.

Are you getting a clear, musical note? If it is muffled or fuzzy you are probably not pressing the string firmly enough.

Second String Songs

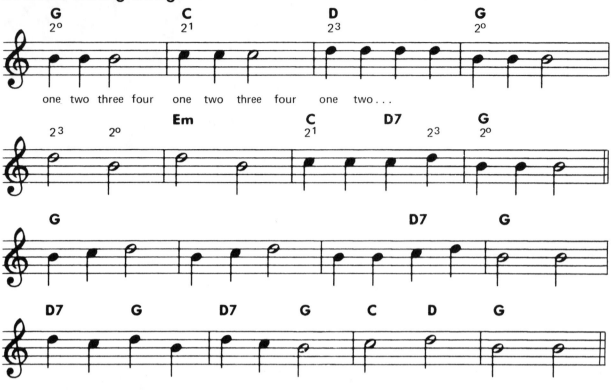

one two three four   one two three four   one two...

Review:
The Notes You've Learned So Far

♩ = 1 beat   ♩ = 2 beats

Two-String Two-Step/For Two Guitars

More Songs On The First Two Strings

Here are some songs that can be played with the notes you know.

Skip To My Lou/With Variations

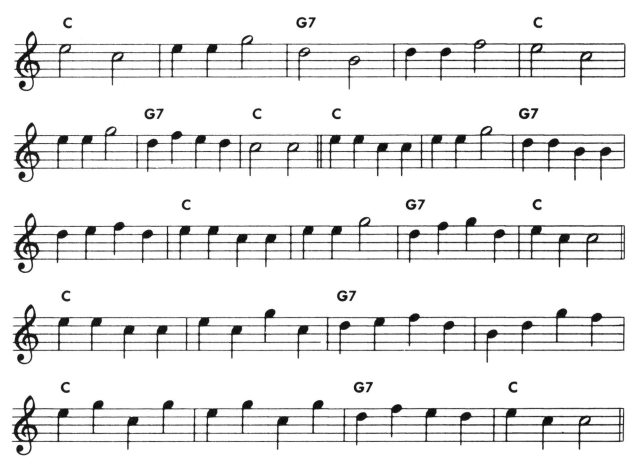

Hint: Press the string firmly against the fingerboard. Use your thumb behind the neck of the guitar to exert the necessary pressure. The fingers should oppose the thumb in a squeezing motion.

Are your fingers getting sore? In time they will develop tough callouses.

White Sand and Gray Sand/A Round for Two Guitars

Rhythm Session: Whole Notes

whole note 𝐨 = 4 beats

Railroad Bill

Notes On The Third String

Playing **G**

The open third string is G (3°).

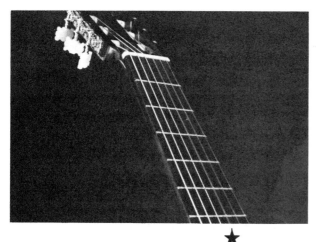

★

Playing **A**

Press the third string behind the second fret to play A (3^2). Use your second finger.

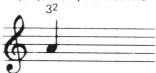

Exercises With **G** And **A**

Review:
The Notes You've Learned So Far

G A B C D E F G └─ one octave ─┘

You now know two different G's, which are one **octave** (eight notes) apart.

Four Folk Songs On Three Strings

Shady Grove

Sinner Man

Yankee Doodle

The Leather-Wing Bat

Music Basics

Time

While you were learning the notes on the first three strings, you may have wondered about some of the other symbols you saw.

The notes are written on five lines called a **staff**:

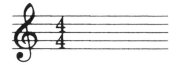 is called the **G clef**, or the **treble clef**. It is a sign that you will see at the beginning of the staff on all guitar music.

The staff is divided into **measures**, which are separated by **bar lines**:

Measures may be made up of quarter notes, half notes, and whole notes, but the total number of beats in each measure is always the same. The **time signature** tells you how many beats there are in each measure.

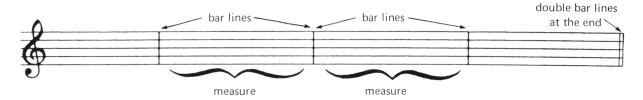

This music is in ⁴⁄₄ time, which means that there are four quarter note beats in each measure.

The top number tells you that there are four beats to each measure.

The bottom number indicates that the beats are quarter notes.

At times we will find music written with other time signatures. When a song is in ¾ time, there are **three** quarter notes in each measure.

count: one two three   one two three   one two three   one two three

Here is a well-known cowboy song in ¾ time.

Streets of Laredo
Cowboy Song

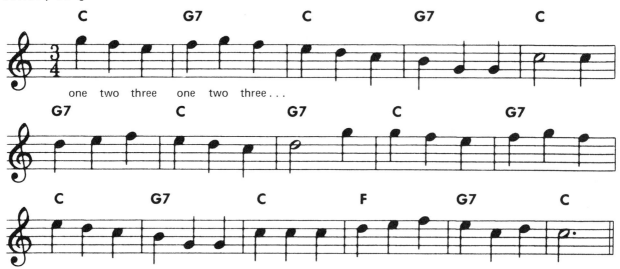

one two three   one two three...

Rhythm Session:
The Dotted Half Note

A note followed by a dot has its time (number of beats) increased by one half. A dotted half note

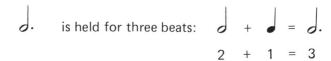

is held for three beats:

2 + 1 = 3

Waltz Around

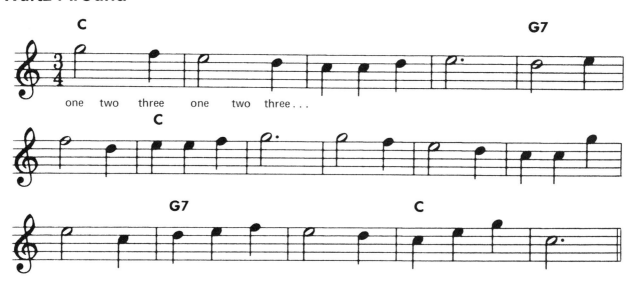

one two three   one two three...

Combining Notes Into Chords

Two or more notes played together are called a **chord**.

Play the following songs and exercises slowly and carefully, strumming in a downward direction on the chords.

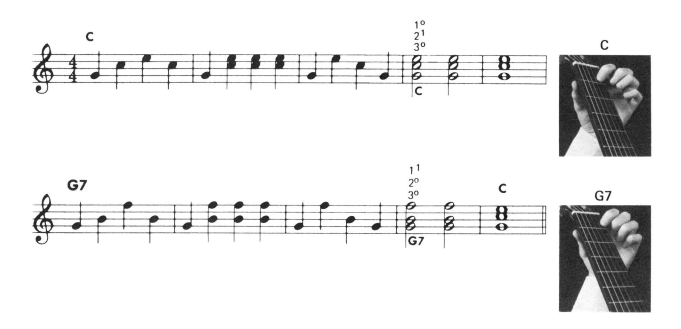

Polka Dots

Mary Ann
Calypso Song

Another Chord Exercise

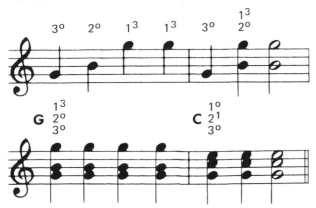

Mexican Dance

I Know Where I'm Going
Old English Folk Song

The Tie

A curved line between two notes on the same line is called a **tie**. When a tie connects two notes, the second note is not picked but held, and its time value is added to the first note.

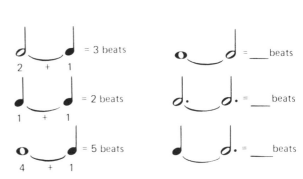

16

Exercise With Two-String Chords

Down In The Valley
American Folk Song

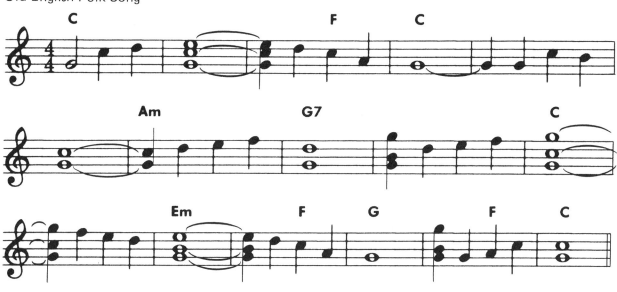

The Water Is Wide
Old English Folk Song

Chord Review

Review:
Writing Your Own Song

Add notes to the measures that are incomplete.
Be sure all measures have the correct number of
beats. Then, learn to play what you have composed.

Title _____ **By** _____

Notes On The Fourth String

Playing D

The open fourth string is D.

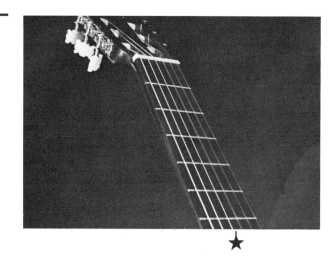

★

Playing E

Fret the fourth string behind the second fret. Use your second finger.

Playing F

Fret the fourth string behind the third fret. Use your third finger.

Fourth String Folly

Groundhog
Mountain Dance Tune

Chord Exercise on 2nd, 3rd and 4th Strings

Deep Blue Sea
Bahamian Song

Rhythm Session:
Eighth Notes

A quarter note can be divided in half, giving you two **eighth notes**.

As you can see, two eighth notes equal one quarter note. Two or more eighth notes are connected by a **beam**.

Techniques And Touches

Alternating Pick Strokes

You will notice that it is difficult to play all these eighth notes with down-strokes. It is easier to alternate your pick strokes so you are picking down ⊓ on the strong beat and up V on the weak beat.

Practice this exercise. Play the down and up strokes smoothly and evenly, with the same tone quality on each.

Joshua Fought the Battle of Jericho
Spiritual

The Pick-Up

A song does not always start on the first beat of the measure. **The Old Chisholm Trail** and **St. James Infirmary** start on the fourth beat. The notes preceding the first full measure are called the **pick-up.** Missing beats from the pick-up measure are found in the last measure of the song.

The Old Chisolm Trail
Cowboy Song

St. James Infirmary
Blues Ballad

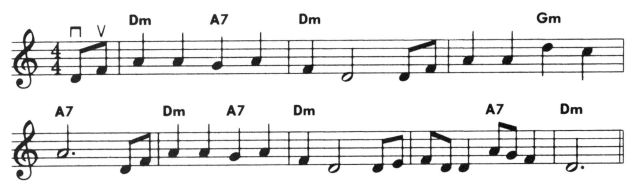

Learn to play this song from memory.

Little Brown Jug
Pioneer Folk Song

The following song has been written with a country-style accompaniment. Learn to play it smoothly, strumming down on the chords without breaking your rhythm.

Pretty Polly
Southern Mountain Ballad

Scarborough Fair
Old English Song

Soleares
Flamenco Dance

Review:
Some Chords You Can Now Play

Notes On The Fifth String

Playing **A**

The open fifth string is A.

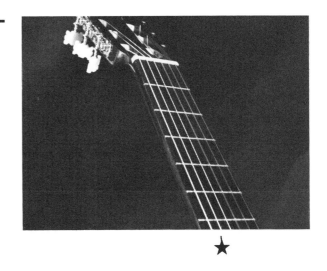

★

Playing **B**

Fret the fifth string behind the second fret. Use your second finger.

Playing **C**

Fret the fifth string behind the third fret. Use your third finger.

Ledger Lines

When the notes are above or below the staff, we add **ledger lines** which represent an extension of the staff. These are the first notes in this book with ledger lines.

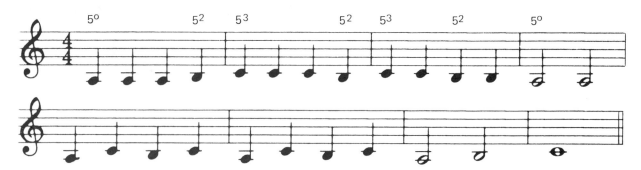

Tumbalalaika
Yiddish Folk Song

Rests

This sign ⅄ is a **quarter note rest**. It tells you to stop playing for one beat.

This is a **half note rest**. ▬ When you see it, pause for two beats. Note that it sits on the third line of the staff.

Count carefully remembering to rest for the correct number of beats.

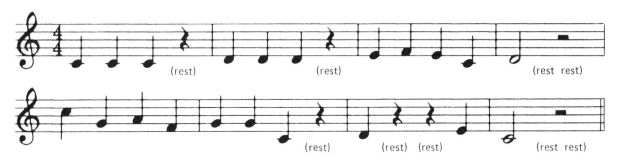

You've Got To Walk That Lonesome Valley

Spiritual

The **whole note rest** ═══ tells you to pause for four beats = a full measure. Note that it hangs from the fourth line of the staff.

Rose/A Round For Two Guitars
Early English Song

Come All You Fair and Tender Ladies
Appalachian Mountain Ballad

The F Chord

The F chord is a little more difficult than the chords you have previously learned because the first **two** strings are held down by the first finger.

Playing The F Chord

Country Songs

In the following songs you will be playing a single bass note followed by a chord. Place your fingers on the bass note and the chord at the same time.

There are still four beats to a measure and they are counted like this:

In these songs, the bass strings are playing the melody, and are shown with the stems down. The chords (stems up) are filling in the rhythm. This is a traditional country sound.

count: one   two   three   four

Country Vamp

Brown Eyes

Wildwood Flower

count one two three four

I Never Will Marry

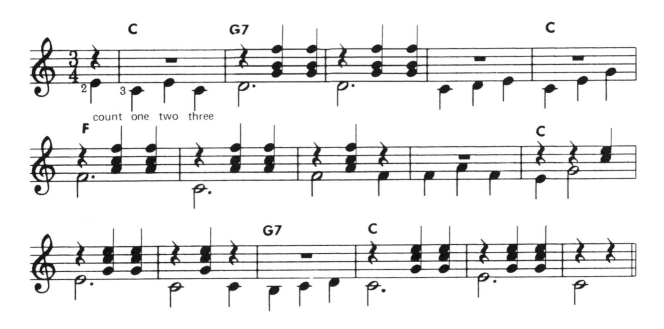

count one two three

Notes On The Sixth String

Playing E

The open sixth string is E, the lowest note on the guitar.

The notes on the sixth, fifth, and fourth strings are called **bass notes**.

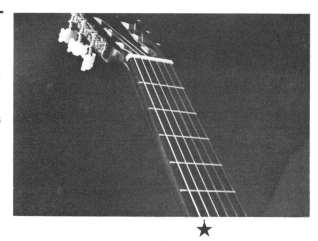

★

Playing F

If you press the sixth string behind the first fret, the note is F. Use your first finger.

Playing G

Press the sixth string behind the third fret to play G. Use your third finger.

Now play this line, using the bass E, F, and G.

Review:
The 17 Notes So Far

Here are the 17 notes we have learned so far.

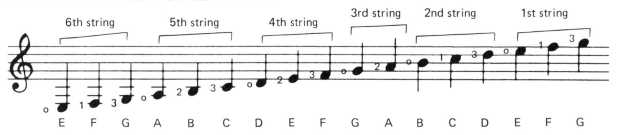

Six-String Exercise

Play this exercise steadily and evenly. With practice you will be able to increase your speed.

God Rest Ye Merry Gentlemen

Dance Of The Goblins

Walking The Basses/Boogie Woogie

Rhythm Session:
Syncopation

These are tied eighth notes. Count this way:

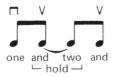

one and two and
└ hold ┘

This change in the accent is called **syncopation.**

Rock Bass

Brandy Leave Me Alone/A Duet

Sevillanas
Traditional Flamenco Dance

Minuet
J.S. Bach

Music Basics

Chord Diagrams

The chords that you have been playing from the music can also be written as **chord diagrams**. Practice these chord positions until you can place your fingers on the notes quickly and accurately.

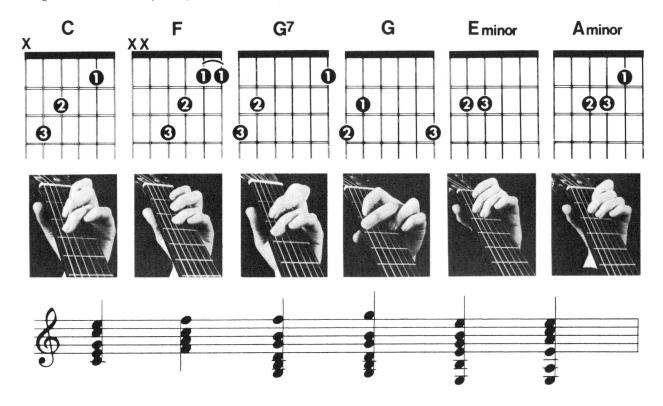

C   F   G7   G   E minor   A minor

/ is another way of saying: strum this chord for one beat.

Strum the chords with a down-stroke, playing very evenly.

Rhythm In Four

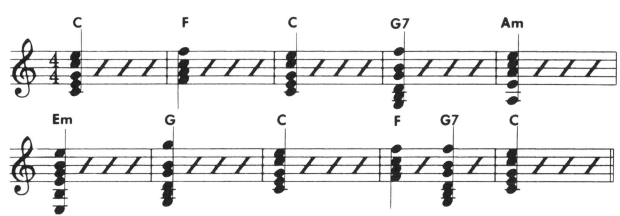

Sharps And Flats

♯ **Sharps** raise a note one half step. To raise a note a half step, play it one fret higher.

♭ **Flats** lower a note one half step. To lower a note a half step, play it one fret lower.

♮ **Naturals** cancel a sharp or flat.

When the same sharp or flat is needed throughout a piece, it is written at the beginning of the staff. This is called the **key signature**.

Be sure that every time you come to an F you raise it one fret to F♯.

House Of The Rising Sun
New Orleans Blues

All My Trials

Bahamian Spiritual

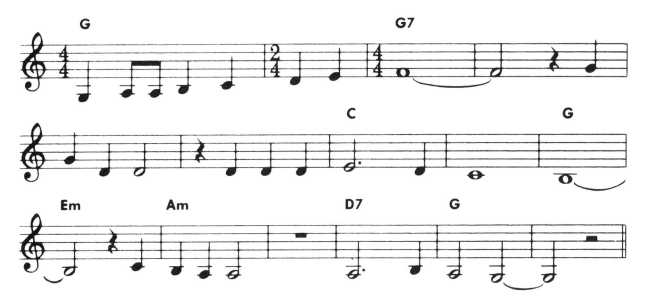

A song will occasionally change its time signature in the middle of the piece. Notice that in **All My Trials** there is one measure of ²⁄₄, although the rest of the song is in ⁴⁄₄ time.

Plaisir D'Amour/Duet

Early French Chanson

Rhythm Session:
Dotted Quarter Notes

A dot after a note increases its time value by one half. Therefore, a **dotted quarter note** is equal to a quarter note plus an eighth note or three eighth notes.

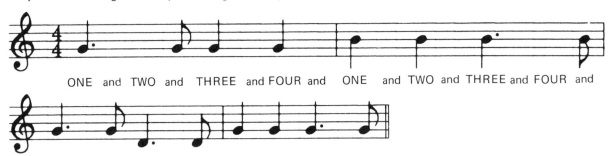

Play the following exercise, counting carefully.

ONE and TWO and THREE and FOUR and   ONE and TWO and THREE and FOUR and

Venezuela
Sea Chantey

Saltarello
Vincenzo Galilei (16th Century Tune)

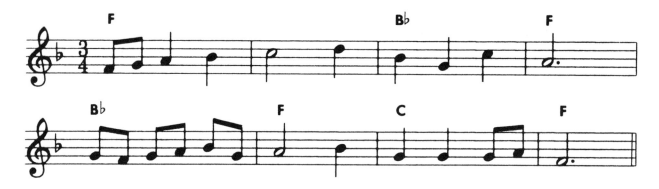

Gavotte
J.S. Bach (arr. Alan de Mause)

Early One Morning
17th Century English Ballad

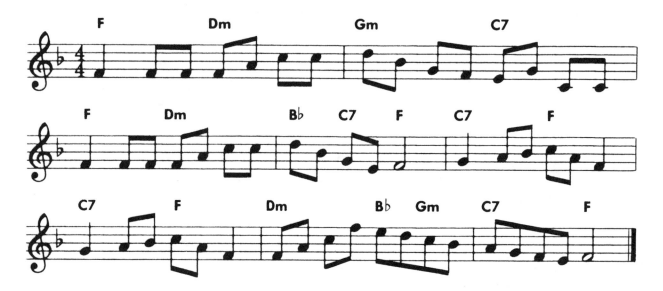

The Little Beggerman

Irish Dance Tune

Every Night When The Sun Goes In

Boogie The Blues!

Tuning Your Guitar

Tightening a string (by turning the appropriate **tuning peg**) will make the **pitch** of that string go up. If you loosen the string, the pitch goes down. This is the way we are able to tune the guitar.

The strings of your guitar should be tuned to these notes:

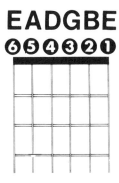

If there is a piano in your house, the same notes look like this:

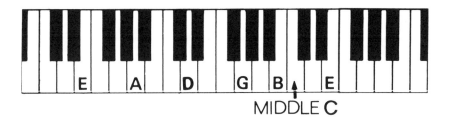

If there is no piano available to give you the correct notes to tune your guitar to, you might buy a guitar pitchpipe, which has the six notes you'll need.

Learning to tune your guitar will take practice and patience. If you find it difficult at first, your teacher will help you until you catch on.

Tuning Without A Piano
Or Pitchpipe

If you do not have a piano or pitchpipe, you can still tune your guitar, since as long as the strings are in tune **relative** to one another, the guitar will sound all right.

Start by getting the 6th string (E) to its approximate pitch. As long as it's not so loose that it makes a buzzing sound, or so tight that it feels stiff and hard to fret, there is no problem.

Fret the 6th string just behind the fifth fret and pluck it with your right hand. That note is the same pitch as your open 5th string (A). Tune the 5th string until the sound matches the 6th string fretted at the fifth fret.

Once the 5th string is in tune, repeat the process by fretting the 5th string just behind the fifth fret. That note should be D, the correct pitch for your open 4th string.

Now your 6th, 5th, and 4th strings should be in tune. Repeat the process by fretting the 4th string at the fifth fret, which will give you the note G, the correct pitch for your open 3rd string.

In order to get your 2nd string in tune, fret the 3rd string behind the **fourth** fret and tune the 2nd string to that note (B).

Finally, fret your 2nd string just behind the fifth fret to get the pitch of your open 1st string (E).

Now your guitar will be in tune, although only to itself, and not necessarily with other instruments.

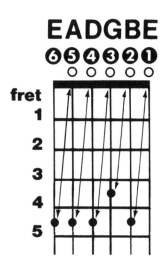

Glossary Of Terms

Here is a list of some important musical terms, in the same order you learned about them in the book.

Pick (plectrum) A small piece of plastic, tortoise shell, metal, or other material used in place of the fingers to pluck the strings.

Frets The thin metal strips spaced along the fingerboard which create the notes of the guitar.

Quarter note ♩ A note which is played for one beat.

Half note ♩ A note which is held for two beats.

Whole note 𝅝 A note which is held for four beats.

Octave Two notes of the same name which are eight notes apart.

Staff The five lines (and spaces) on which the musical notes are written.

G Clef (treble clef) 𝄞 The sign placed at the beginning of each staff of guitar music.

Measures The spaces between the bar lines, dividing the staff into equal sections.

Bar lines The vertical lines demarking the measures on the musical staff.

Time Signature The sign or fraction placed at the beginning of a musical piece to indicate how you count the music. The top number tells you how many beats will be in each measure, and the bottom number tells you what kind of beats they are.

Waltz Time Music written with a time signature of ¾.

Dotted half note ♩. A note equal to three beats.

Chords Chords are made up of a combination of two or more notes played together.

Tie A curved line between two notes of the same pitch indicating that the time value of the second note is added to the first.

Eighth note ♪ A note with a time value of half a quarter note.

Beam ♫ The line which connects two or more eighth notes.

Pick-up The notes preceding the first complete measure of a musical piece.

Ledger lines The short lines added to notes which are written above or below the regular staff.

Quarter note rest 𝄽 The sign indicating a pause of one beat.

Half note rest ▬ Indicates a pause of two beats.

Whole note rest ▬ Pause for four beats.

Syncopation The change of accent in the rhythm of a piece of music to the weaker beat. This is often achieved by the use of tied eighth notes.

Tied eighth notes A series of eighth notes in which the second of two eighth notes is tied to the first of the next two eighth notes.

Chord diagram A sort of map of the fingerboard showing where the fingers are placed in order to play a given chord.

Sharp ♯ A sign indicating that a note is to be raised one fret (a half step).

Flat ♭ A sign which indicates that a note is to be lowered one fret (one half step).

Natural ♮ A natural cancels a previous sharp or flat.

Key signature Sharp or flat signs placed after the G clef indicating that certain notes are to be played sharp or flat throughout the piece. The number of sharp or flat signs tell you which key the music is in. (See Vol. 2 for a more complete discussion of keys.)

Dotted quarter notes ♩. These notes are equal to a quarter plus an eighth, or three eighth notes.

CONGRATULATIONS!

Now that you have completed this book and have learned to play the songs in it, you are ready to go on to Book 2.

In the second book we will continue our exploration of the guitar fingerboard, while building your strength, speed, and technique.

In addition to note reading, Book 2 will start you on chords and accompaniment patterns for a wide variety of music.

Play guitar with Happy Traum.
Basic Guitar Lessons.

Book Two.

To the Teacher

This book, the second in a series of four volumes, continues the study of the guitar in much the same style and method as the first. It is my belief that the student will learn eagerly when he is playing music that he enjoys right from the earliest lessons. Therefore, I have taught note-reading, chord theory, and right and left hand technique with the emphasis on repertoire. Scales and exercises are kept to a minimum except when they are necessary to bring the student to the next step. By using popular, folk, bluegrass, and blues songs, as well as some material from the classical repertoire, the student will become a well-rounded guitarist and hopefully, a musically educated one.

As in the first book, it is important that the teacher work closely with the student, guiding him or her and supplementing the text with his or her own knowledge and ideas. I have included several duets, and accompaniment chords have been provided in the belief that the student must play with others to get the full benefit of the instrument.

Once again, this book can be thought of as a guideline into which the creative teacher can bring his own ideas and teaching style, supplementing the material with his or her own to give the student the fullest experience possible.

To the Student

You have completed the first book and are about to start on the second, so you should no longer think of yourself as a beginner. You will be moving into new areas and developing new skills and techniques that will be both challenging and rewarding. As you work your way through this volume, try to be aware of playing more than just the notes. You are becoming a musician now, and you should be aware of making *music* with each new piece you play.

There are many different playing styles illustrated in these pages, and hopefully some of them will touch on the kind of music you have been wanting to play. More important, though, you will be playing and learning forms and styles that will open *new* areas of interest for you.

Play the songs, instrumentals, and exercises in this book carefully, making certain that you have mastered one technique before going on to the next. Memorize the songs you like and play them for your friends. This will give you a goal to work toward, and the pleasure your playing imparts to others will surely spur you on to new challenges and accomplishments.

Good luck!
Happy Traum

Copyright © 1976 Acorn Music Press
Published 1984 by Amsco Publications,
A Division of Music Sales Corporation, New York
All Rights Reserved

Order No. AM 34919
US International Standard Book Number: 0.8256.2357.X
UK International Standard Book Number: 0.7119.0438.3
Library of Congress Catalog Card Number: 75-32886

Exclusive Distributors:
Music Sales Corporation
257 Park Avenue South, New York, NY 10010 USA
Music Sales Limited
8/9 Frith Street, London W1V 5TZ England
Music Sales Pty. Limited
120 Rothschild Street, Rosebery, Sydney, NSW 2018, Australia

The Author would like to thank Alan de Mause for his invaluable
contribution of ideas and material in the presentation of this book.

Printed in the United States of America by
Vicks Lithograph and Printing Corporation

Amsco Publications
New York/London/Sydney

Notes For Review

All The Notes You Know So Far

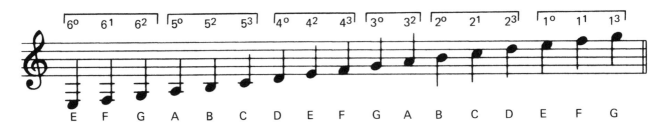

Time Values

Quarter note ♩ = one beat

Half note ♩ = two beats

Dotted half note ♩. = three beats

Whole note 𝐨 = four beats

Eighth note ♪ = half a beat

Dotted quarter note ♩. = one and a half beats

Sharps, Flats And Naturals

A **sharp** sign ♯ raises a note by one fret (one half step).

A **flat** sign ♭ lowers a note by one fret (one half step).

A **natural** sign ♮ cancels a previous sharp or flat sign.

Songs For Review

The Key Of C

No sharps or flats.

Reminder: ⊓ = pick down   V = pick up

Come Follow

In The Good Old Colony Days

Early American Song

*Chord names are for teacher accompaniment.

3

The Keeper (duet*)

Old English Song

*The student should learn both parts of all duets in this book.

Chords For Review

Here Are The Chords You Know So Far

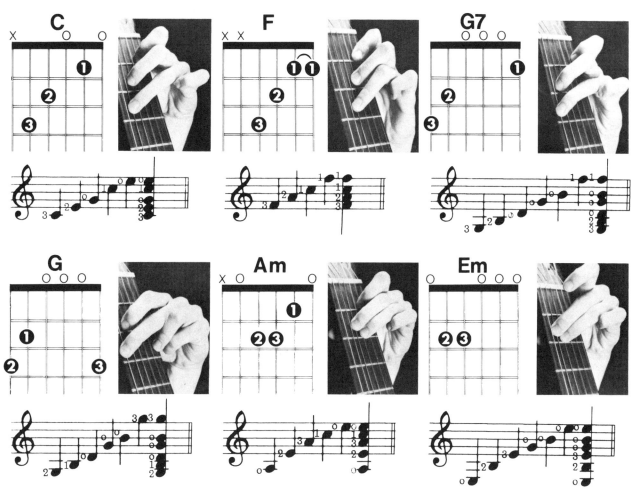

Play slowly and carefully.

Playing Rhythm Chords

Strum down (⊓) across the strings to play the
chord rhythm where you see this mark / .

Learn to play both the rhythm and the solo parts.

Kilgary Mountain

Slow and steady

Playing Melody With Chord Accompaniment:
Solo

Reminder: The bass notes (stems down) are the melody. The chords (stems up) provide the accompaniment.

Wherever possible, fret the bass note and the chord at the same time.

Hard Ain't It Hard

count: 1 2 3 4

Hint: Keep the nails on your left hand cut short so they do not interfere with pressing the strings firmly to the fingerboard.

Old Rosin The Bow

This is a good piece to learn to play from memory.
When you feel you know it, play it for your family
and friends.

Irish Folk Song

*The double line here marks the end of a section. The heavier line
indicates the end of the piece.

Hint: Some guitarists get a sharper bass note by
plucking the string straight down and letting the
pick come to rest on the next string. Try it.

8

Playing Scales

A scale is a series of notes going up or down in alphabetical order, beginning and ending with the same note an octave apart.

The Key Of C Major

The **C major scale** has no sharps or flats. It is made up entirely of natural notes (♮).

The Key Of G Major

The **G major scale** has one sharp (F♯) in its key signature. Here are two places to play the scale.

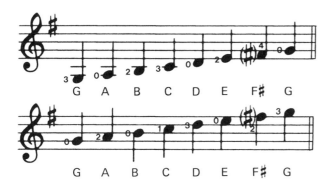

The Key Of F Major

The **F major scale** has one flat (B♭) in its key signature. Here are two places to play the F major scale.

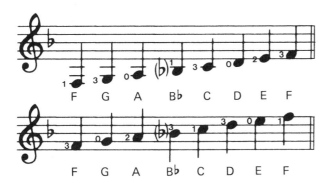

Playing In The Key Of G

Reminder: There is an F♯ in the key signature.

Andante In G

Fernando Sor
1778-1839

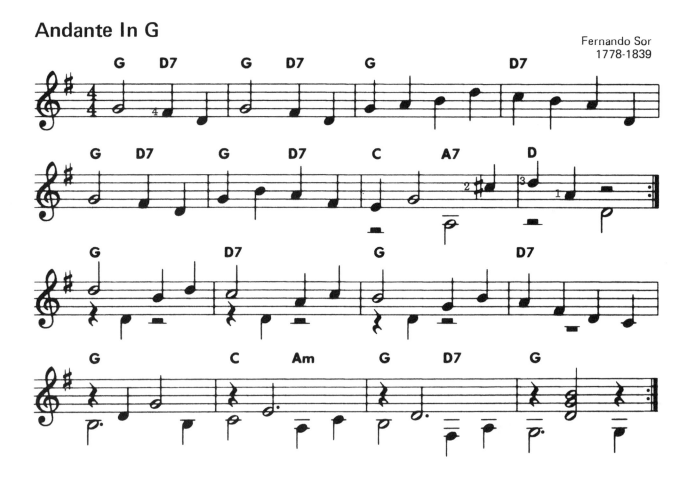

Theme From Lagrima

Francisco Tárrega
1854-1909

Playing Melody With Chord Accompaniment In G

The basic chords in the key of G are G, C, and D7. D7 is the only one you haven't learned so far. Here it is:

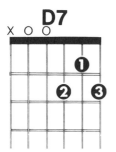

I Am A Pilgrim

I am a pil - grim, and a stran - ger, a trav' - lin' through this wear - y land, I got a home in that yon - der cit - y, Good Lord, and it's not (oh Lord it's not) not made by man.

Yellow Bird

West Indian Folk Song

Reminder: The second of two tied notes is sustained but not struck again.

Allegro

Anon. (Renaissance)

12

Playing In The Key Of F

Reminder: There is a B♭ in the key signature.

O No John!

J. S. Bach

Gavotte

Minuet In F

Antonio Diabelli
1781-1858

D.C. (Da Capo) tells you to go back to the beginning of the piece.

Fine marks the end of the piece.

D.C. al Fine means that you go back to the beginning and play until the sign **Fine**.

Playing High A

Using your fourth finger, press behind the fift
fret on the first string (1⁵) to play high A.

Since this note is above the staff, it is written with
a ledger line.

Black Is The Color Of My True Love's Hair

Black black black is the co-lor of my true love's hair_____ Her cheeks

are some-thing won-drous fair_____ the_ pur-est eyes and the dain-ti-est

hands I love _____ the ground on which she stands._____

*Notice that the time signature is $\frac{2}{4}$, or two quarter notes per
measure.

Paddy West

Chord Review:
Harmonizing A Song

Directions: Fill in chord notes below the melody as in the first measure. Use the chord symbol as your guide. Make sure that the existing melody remains as the highest note ih your arrangement.

One possible solution:

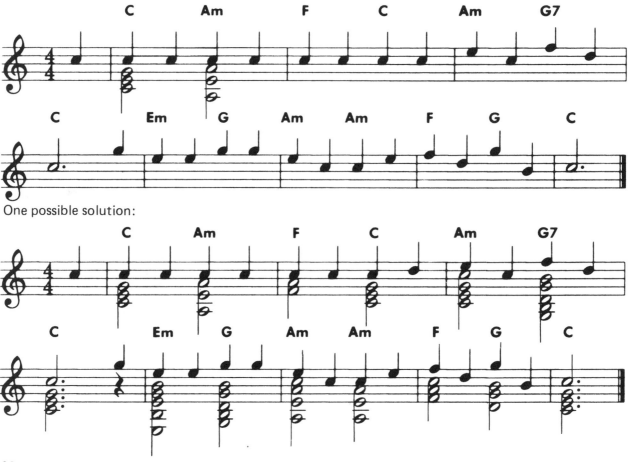

16

Two Bluegrass Breakdowns

Practice for development of speed and pick technique.

Turkey In The Straw

American Folk Song

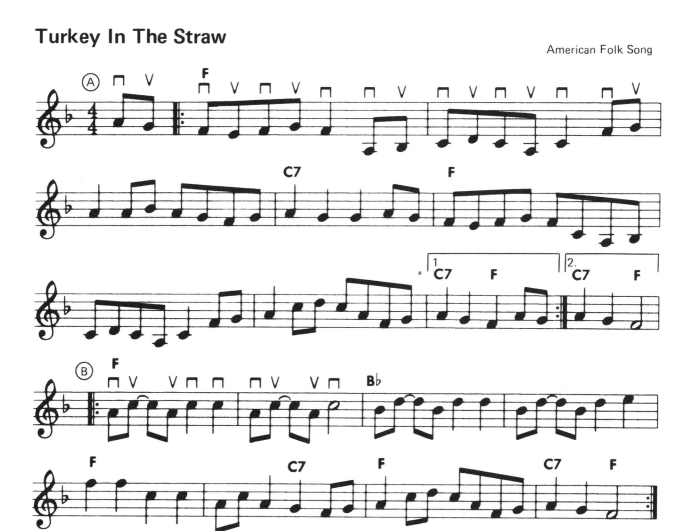

*First and second endings: This sign ‖: :‖ tells you to repeat everything between the dots. Play to the first dotted double line. After repeating the section, skip the measure marked ⌐1.⌐ and play the second ending ⌐2.⌐ . Then proceed to the next part of the song. The B section is also repeated once in its entirety.

Arkansas Traveller

Some Musical Terms
You Should Know

Allegro Fast

Andante Moderate (a walking speed)

Lento Slow

Forte (f) Loud

Mezzo Forte (mf) Moderately Loud

Piano (p) Soft

Mezzo Piano (mp) Moderately Soft

Ritardando (rit.) Retard, gradually slowing down

A Tempo Return to original speed

Rhythm Session:
$\frac{6}{8}$ Time

$\frac{6}{8}$ time indicates six eighth notes in each measure. The beats are counted in groups of three, with the accent on the first of each three notes:

Dotted quarter notes are frequently used, giving the equivalent time of three eighth notes:

This strong, bouncy rhythm, often heard in songs of European origin, has a very different effect than either $\frac{3}{4}$ or $\frac{4}{4}$ time.

Tarantella

Popular Italian Dance

The Irish Washerwoman

Note the picking pattern, which emphasizes the first of each group of three notes.

Irish Jig

Away Rio

Sea Chantey

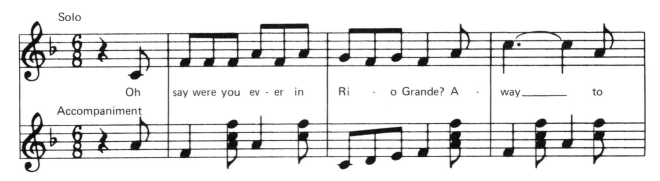

Oh say were you ev - er in Ri - o Grande? A - way_____ to

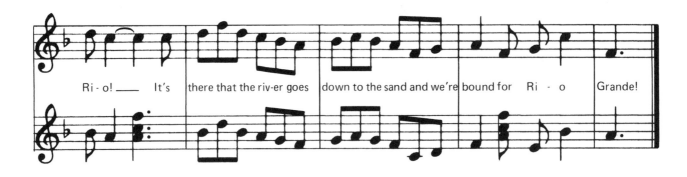

Ri - o!_____ It's there that the riv-er goes down to the sand and we're bound for Ri - o Grande!

Work Sheet:
Addition In $\frac{6}{8}$ Time

A $\frac{6}{8}$ ♪ + ♪ + ♪ = ___ How many beats?

(Think: 1 + 1 + 1 = ___)

B $\frac{6}{8}$ ♩. + ♪ = ___

C $\frac{6}{8}$ ♫♫ + 𝄽 = ___

D $\frac{6}{8}$ ♪ + ♩ + ♩. = ___

E ♩ + ♩ + ♪ = ___

F ♩ + ♫♫ + ♪ = ___

G ♫ + ♩ = ___

Answers: A/3 B/4 C/5 D/6 E/5 F/6 G/4

Playing Arpeggios

The term **arpeggio** means "harp-like" in Italian, and is used when chords are broken up into their separate notes. This technique is often used for accompanying melodies.

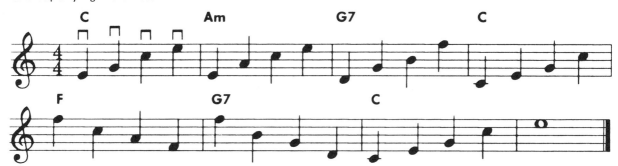

Hold the notes of the arpeggio down so they ring together for each entire measure.

Mary Hamilton

The Butterfly

Mauro Giuliani
1781-1829

Andante

* ⅞ is an eighth note rest. Pause for a half beat.

Playing In Minor Keys

Play the C scale.

Now play it again, this time beginning and ending on A.

The relative minor of C major is A minor.

Minor scales begin on the 6th note of the major scale. Since the major and minor scales are related to one another by having the same key signature, they are called "relative" scales.

The relative minor of G major is E minor:

When you play these scales you will hear that they sound very different. The reason that the minor key sounds the way it does is that the pattern of whole-steps and half-steps has been altered. Compare the patterns of the two related scales.

Sometimes the sixth and/or seventh notes of the minor scale are raised, bringing it closer in sound to the major scale. As long as the half-step is between the second and third notes of the scale, however, it will have a minor sound.

The previous minor scales are called **natural** minors. These new examples are called **harmonic** minor scales. Note that the key signatures for both types of minor scales are the same even though the harmonic minor contains the raised seventh. This is always written as an accidental as it occurs.

Compare these two versions of the same song, one in major and the other in the relative harmonic minor.

Down In The Valley (major)

Down in the val - ley, _____ the val - ley so low. _____

Hang your head o - ver _____ hear the wind blow. _____

Down In The Valley (relative harmonic minor)

Basic Chords In A Minor

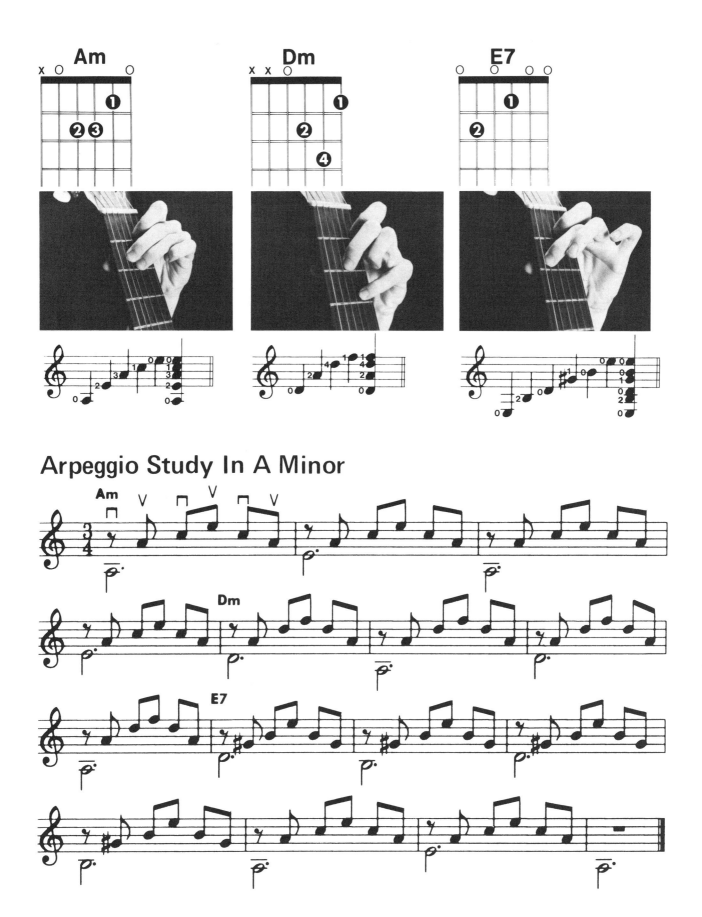

Arpeggio Study In A Minor

Let My People Go

American Slave Song

* This sign ⌢ is a **fermata**. Hold the note under it slightly longer than usual.

900 Miles

Railroad Ballad

Chord Practice:
Key Of A Minor

Practice for development of speed and accuracy.

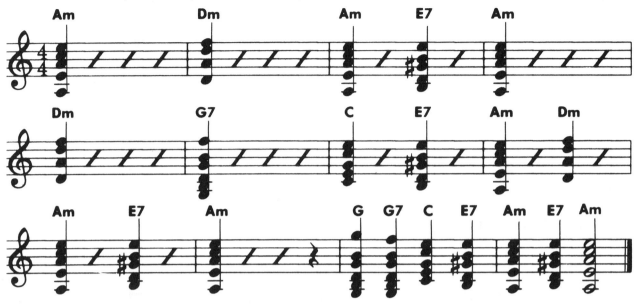

Arpeggios In A Minor In $\frac{6}{8}$ Time

Play evenly at your own speed.

Now write your own $\frac{6}{8}$ patterns using the chords shown below.

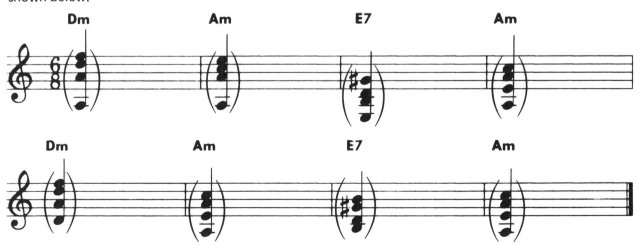

Basic Chords In E Minor

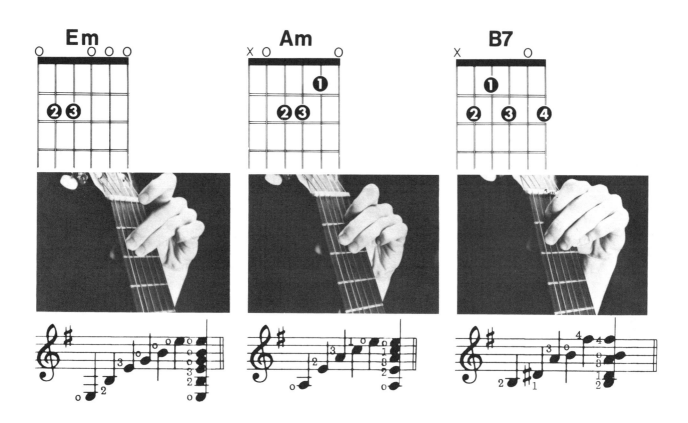

Arpeggio Study In E Minor

Keep Your Hand On That Plow

Spiritual

30

Chord Practice:
Key Of E Minor

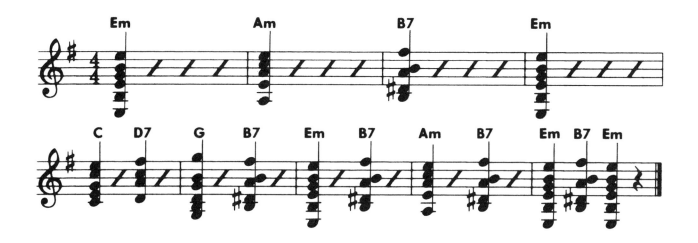

Moscow Nights

Russian Popular Song

Rhythm Session:
Triplets

A **triplet** is a group of three eighth notes which are played to a count equal to one beat.

count: TRIP - a - let TRIP - a - let TRIP - a - let TRIP - a - let

Sometimes the first two beats of the triplet are tied. It is then counted this way:

TRIP (A) let

The following melody by Johann S. Bach is an excellent piece with which to strengthen both your left and right hands, and improve your understanding of playing triplets.

Jesu, Joy Of Man's Desiring

J. S. Bach

Triplet Rock

Flamenco Variation On Soleares

Playing In The Key Of D

The key of D has two sharps, F♯ and C♯.

My Creole Belle

American Parlor Song

My Cre - ole Belle   I love her well ____ My dar - lin' ba - by,

My Cre - ole   Belle.   When stars do   shine ____ I'll call her

mine. ____   My dar - lin' ba - by,   My Cre - ole Belle. _____

Early One Morning (with variation)

English Folk Song

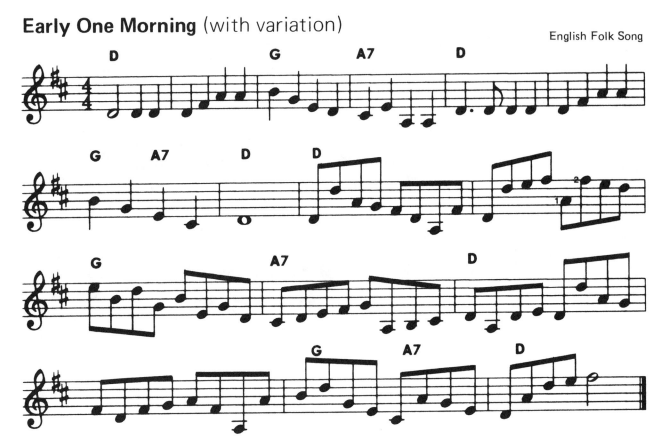

Frankie And Johnny Blues

Reminder: Syncopated tied eighth notes are counted this way:

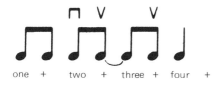

one + two + three + four +

The Nightingale

Old English Song

Playing Chords In D

The basic chords in the key of D are D, G, and A7.

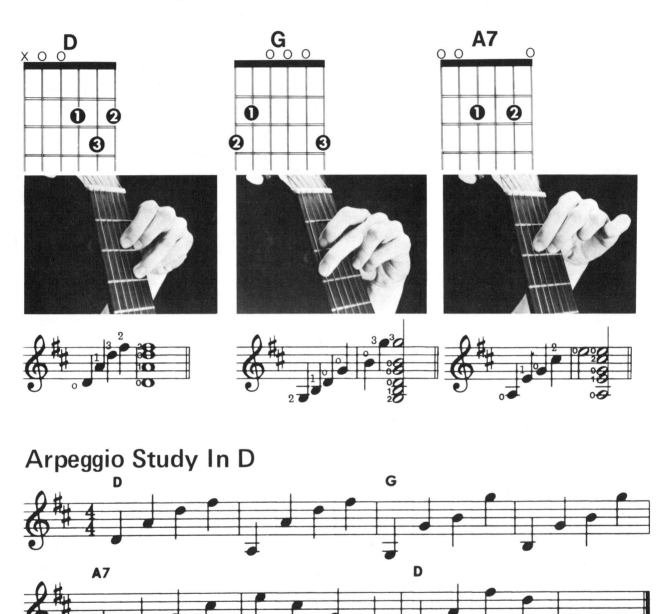

Arpeggio Study In D

Bass-Chord Accompaniment Pattern In D

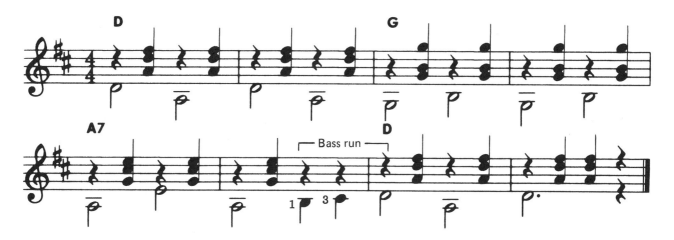

A series of bass notes leading into a new chord is called a **bass run**.

The Waltzing Bass Runner

The **bass run** provides interest, and often harmonizes with the melody you are accompanying.

The Frozen Logger

Playing Rhythm Guitar

Now that you are familiar with some of the basic chords, you can put them to further use by learning some rhythmic strums. These rhythms are used to accompany melodies, either sung or played by another instrument.

Play each pattern over and over until it flows freely. It is important that you learn to change chords without hesitating so that the rhythm is smooth and even.

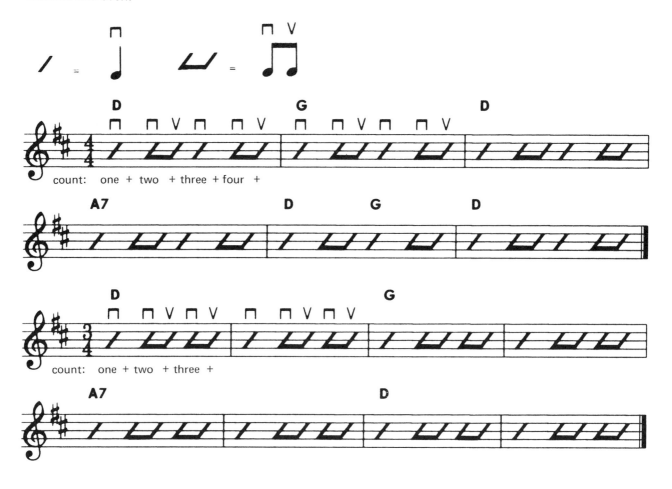

Hint: Brush the pick **lightly** across the strings. The up-stroke need only be played on the first two or three strings.

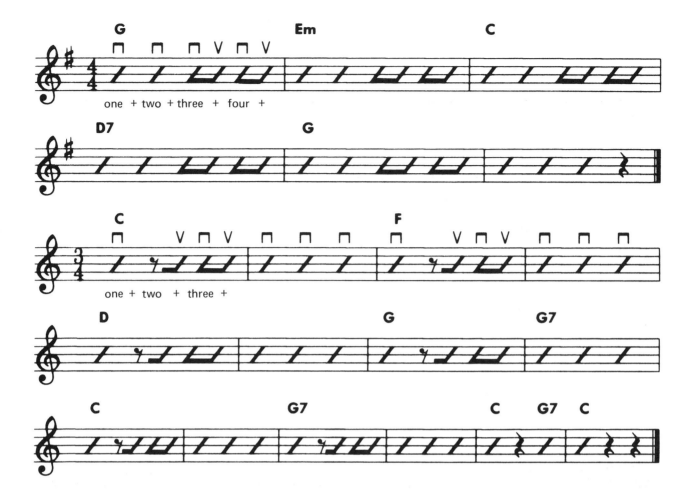

Be careful in avoiding strumming all six strings on every chord. For instance, make sure you are not accidentally striking the sixth string on the F or B^7 chord.

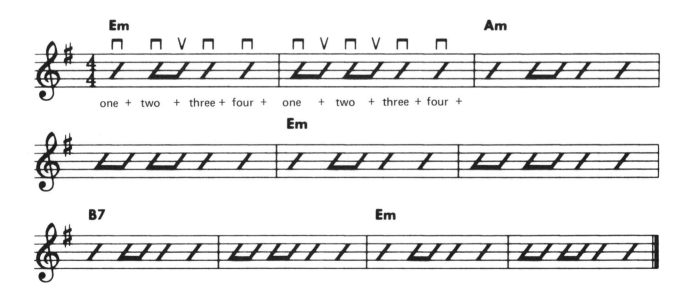

Hints: Your wrist and forearm should be as loose and relaxed as possible. Don't grip the pick too tightly. Get into the rhythm you are playing.

Country Rhythm:
The Bluegrass Strum

Practice the following bass-chord pattern until it is smooth and easy. Pay special attention to your pick direction.

When you play this rhythm, your bass notes should be sharp and clean. Try picking near the bridge for a sharper sound. Let the pick glide lightly over the chords.

She'll Be Comin' Round The Mountain

Playing The Calypso Rhythm

Practice the following rhythm pattern until it is
very smooth. Then try it with the songs below.

Pay Me My Money Down

Bahaman Folk Song

Reminder: Count the **syncopated** notes this way:

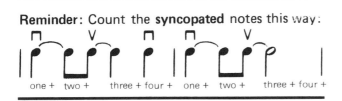

Graduation Recital

Now is the time to congratulate yourself for having made it through the book. Play these recital pieces for your friends!

Spanish Dance

This makes an excellent second chorus to the blues
on p. 35. Watch the accidentals.

Variation On Frankie And Johnny Blues

Jamaica Farewell

Calypso Folk Song

If you play this as a duet, have your partner play an accompaniment using the calypso strum introduced on the previous page.

Chord Chart Of Major, Dominant 7th And Minor Chords

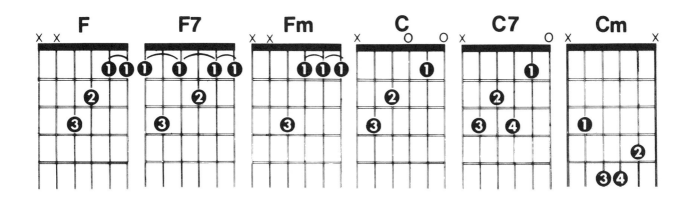

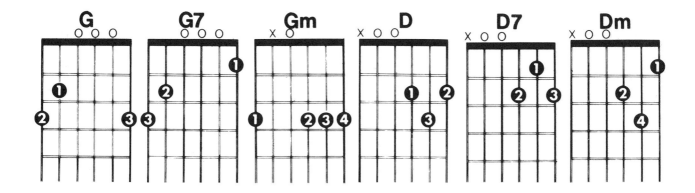

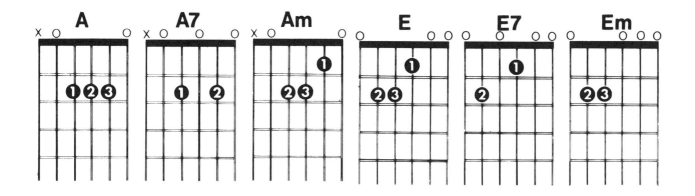

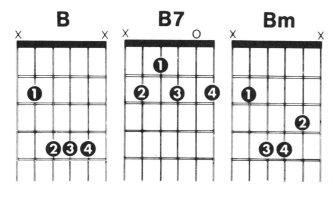

Explanation: This chart includes all of the chords you have studied **plus** any additional major, dominant 7th, or minor chord with the same letter name. For instance, B7 is the only B type chord you have studied so far, and the chart also includes B and Bm.

CONGRATULATIONS!

You have completed Book Two, and mastered many important skills of the learning guitarist. You will find that it is both rewarding and fun to play what you have learned for your family and friends.

In Basic Lessons Book Three, we will continue to study new keys, chords, and techniques—including an exploration of finger-style guitar, which will open up many new music possibilities for you.

Play guitar with Happy Traum.
Basic Guitar Lessons.
Book Three.

In Basic Guitar Lessons 1 and 2 we explored many of the beginning techniques of guitar playing, while working towards an understanding of the fundamentals of music. Book 3 continues where the others leave off, but with a new direction — finger-style playing. If you have completed the first two books, you should have no trouble getting into this one. If you have not studied the other Basic Guitar Lessons, but play some guitar and would like to start your studies with this book, look over the brief review on the next page. This will give you an idea of the level at which you will need to be in order to get the maximum benefit from Book 3.

As you work your way through this volume you will find that the many songs, rounds, solos and duets will provide you with a working repertoire as well as a variety of techniques for use in many kinds of music. By the time you have finished, you will have had experience playing some folk, classical, blues and even flamenco, which will help you to become a well-rounded and accomplished player. Of course, a good teacher, some determination and a lot of serious work will all help you to get the most out of these lessons, but the most important thing is to make good music. That will be your ultimate goal.

Good luck!
Happy Traum

Copyright © 1976 by Acorn Music Press,
Published 1984 by Amsco Publications,
A Division of Music Sales Corporation, New York, NY.

International Standard Book Number: 0.8256.2358.8
Library of Congress Catalog Card Number: 75-32886

Exclusive Distributors:
Music Sales Corporation
24 East 22nd Street, New York, NY 10010 USA
Music Sales Limited
8/9 Frith Street, London W1V 5TZ England
Music Sales Pty. Limited
120 Rothschild Street, Rosebery, Sydney, NSW 2018, Australia

The author would like to thank Alan de Mause for his invaluable
contribution of ideas and material in the preparation of this book.

Printed in the United States of America by
Vicks Lithograph and Printing Corporation

Amsco Publications
London/New York/Sydney

Review

In Books 1 and 2 we have worked with twelve basic chords. These positions should be easy and natural by now. If you cannot make the chord changes easily, practice until you can do them smoothly and quickly.

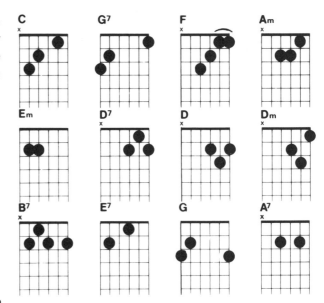

We have played scales and instrumentals in four major keys: **C, G, F** and **D**.

We learned to read single note melodies, chords and combinations of the two. All playing was done with the flatpick.

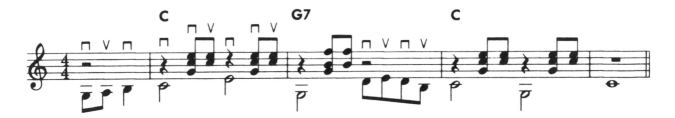

We learned much more in the first two books, but if you feel comfortable with these techniques, I think you will be ready to go on to Book 3.

Playing Finger-Style Guitar

In the first two books of Basic Guitar Lessons we worked on plectrum or pick-style guitar playing. Many guitarists however, use their fingers to pluck or strum the strings. This opens up a whole new style with many other possibilities. Since a good guitarist should become proficient in all types of playing, I will devote this volume to finger-style guitar techniques.

The fingers of the right hand are assigned letters:

T = thumb; **I** = index; **M** = middle; **R** = **ring***

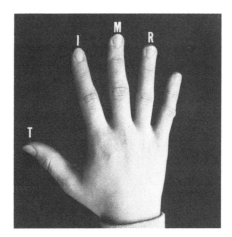

For many standard accompaniment styles, the thumb plucks the 6th, 5th, and 4th strings (the bass notes).

The index finger plucks the 3rd string, the middle finger plucks the 2nd string, and the ring finger plucks the 1st string.

(Sometimes this is not the case, so watch the fingering notation.)

*In the classical guitar method, the fingers are designated with the Spanish letters: p = thumb; i = index; m = middle; a = ring.

The Free Stroke

Rest your thumb temporarily on the 6th string to position your hand. With the tip of your index finger, pluck the 3rd string towards the palm of your hand. Do not hit any of the other strings while doing this.

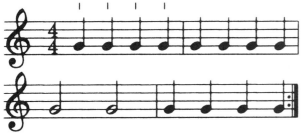

With a similar motion, pluck the 2nd string with your middle finger. Relax your right hand as much as possible.

Pluck the 1st string with your ring finger. Stroke the string. Don't grab it with your finger as this will give you a slapping sound when you release it.

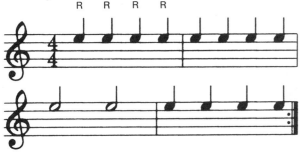

Next, move your three fingers as a group, picking the first three strings simultaneously. You are now plucking a chord.

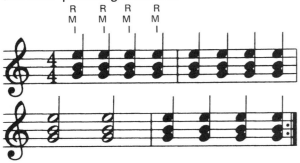

Note: The terms **picking, plucking, stroking,** and **striking** can all be used to describe what you do to make the string sound, and are interchangeable.

The Thumb

The first three fingers rest in their positions for picking the first three strings. Pluck the 6th string with the outer edge of your thumb-tip and nail, using a downward motion but with just enough of an angle so that you clear the 5th string.

Try the same thing with the 5th and 4th strings. Hold your thumb in such a way that it does not collide with your index finger.

Hint: When playing finger-style guitar, the nails on your right hand can be very important in achieving the right tone, volume, and clarity. They should be one sixteenth to one eighth inch longer than the tip of each finger, and filed to follow the same oval shape as the finger-tip. Keep them neat and try not to break them. The nails on your left hand should be kept short.

The **free stroke** means that after plucking a note, your thumb or fingers do not touch any of the neighboring strings.

Right Hand Exercises

Play these exercises until you can pluck the strings smoothly and accurately. Start slowly in order to maintain an even tempo.

Use your thumb to play the following bass notes:

Combine bass notes and chords:

Check List

Is your right hand relaxed? If it is too tense you will not be able to pluck the notes smoothly.

When plucking, do the strings smack against the frets? If so, you are pulling the strings in an outward direction. Stroke in the direction of the 6th string.

Is your thumb bumping into your index finger? Place it well away from the rest of the fingers in its own playing area.

The Bass-Chord Combination

Alternating bass notes with chords provides a good basic rhythm for accompanying many songs. The bass notes are plucked with the thumb, while the chord is picked with the index, middle, and ring fingers.

Hint: Be sure that each finger plucks only its own string.

Play the following songs as a duet with your teacher or a friend.

The Range Rider
Happy Traum

For songs in ¾ time, the pattern will be
BASS-CHORD-CHORD:

Example: **G**

On Top Of Old Smokey

Folk Song

On top of old Smo key____

____ All cov - ered with snow____

I lost my true lov - er____

____ From a - court - in' too slow.____

Playing Arpeggios

The term **arpeggio** is used when chords are broken up into their separate notes. This technique is often used for accompanying melodies.

Hold the entire chord for each measure. This will allow the notes to ring out.

Reminder: Notes with stems down are played with the thumb.

You've learned the left hand fingering for these chords in Books 1 and 2, so concentrate on your right hand.

Rainy Day

It's important that these exercises flow smoothly, so play them slowly at first, gradually increasing your speed.

Come Along

April Song

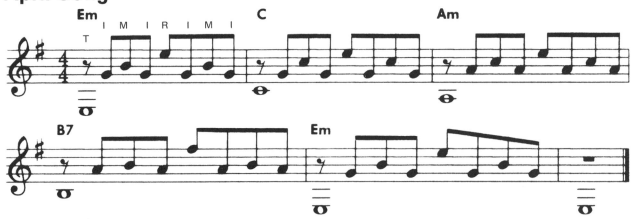

Finger-Hopping

Using Arpeggios For Song Accompaniment

The songs below use one or more of the arpeggios you have learned to provide the accompaniment. The melody can either be played on a second guitar or sung.

Arpeggio:

Barbara Allen
Old English Ballad

In Scar-let Town where I was born, There was a
fair maid dwell-in'___ Made ev-'ry youth___ cry
"Well a - day", Her name was__ Bar - b'ra Al - len.__

Arpeggio:

Greensleeves
Elizabethan Ballad

A - las my love you___ do me wrong to___ cast me out so dis - cour - teous - ly, For I have lov - ed you so long, de - light - ing in_____ your com - pa - ny.

Playing In The Key Of D Minor

The relative minor of F major is D minor.*

Basic Chords In D Minor

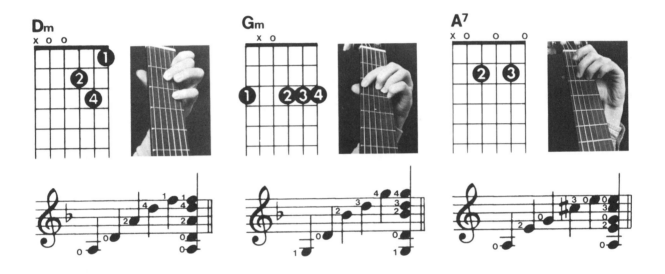

Arpeggio Study In D Minor

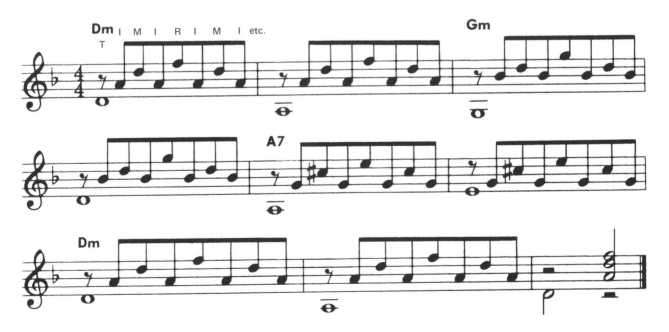

*Relative major and minor keys have been discussed in Book
2, page 23.

The Three Ravens
Old English Ballad

Chord Progressions

The chords in the following songs repeat over and over. This pattern is called a **chord progression.**

Many songs are based on the same chord progression. In this example, the bass notes form a pattern of their own.

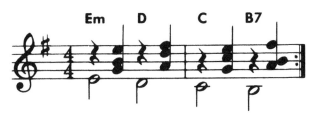

Hey, Ho, Nobody Home
English Round

This well-known song follows the same chord progression. The melody can also be played or sung as a round. The chords will fit right in either way.

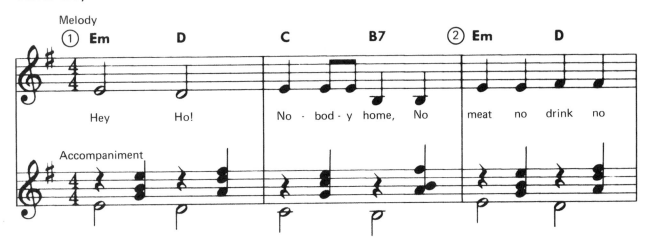

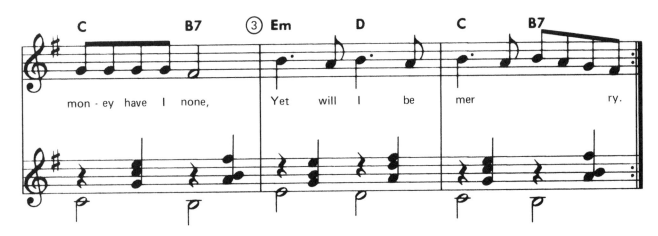

This chord progression can also be played in A minor. Compare this with the one above.

Go back and look at *Greensleeves* again. You will see that the accompaniment follows the same chord progression.

Here is another well-known chord progression:

These chords are the basis for many rock songs of the fifties. Playing it this way will make it sound even more familiar.

Fifties Rock

Play the next song as a duet. Play the chord progression and arpeggio above while your teacher plays the melody. Then switch parts.

The Greaser

Molly Malone

Irish Folk Song

This song can be played with the same chord progression as *The Greaser.* Use a new arpeggio.

Solo Playing:
Melody With Accompaniment

In the following guitar solos, the bass notes play the melody of the song while the index, middle, and ring fingers provide chord and arpeggio accompaniment.

The Rest Stroke

To emphasize the bass notes, your thumb can play a **rest stroke.** Pluck the string so that your thumb comes to rest on the next string. This will give you a sharper, clearer, and slightly louder bass note.

Etude In D Minor

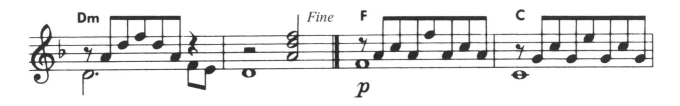

All The Pretty Little Horses

Early American Lullaby

It is sometimes necessary to use your thumb to play the higher strings. Watch the fingering carefully.

Wilson's Wilde

John Dowland
Arr. Alan de Mause

Once again, the thumb plays the 3rd string as well as the lower bass notes to emphasize the melody. The index and middle fingers also change strings, so read carefully.

Review:
Tempo Markings

Tempo markings, found at the beginning of a piece of music, give a general indication of the speed with which a piece should be played. Some of the most commonly used terms are:

Allegro—Fast, happy
Andante—At a moderate, walking speed
Moderato—At a moderate pace
Lento—Slowly

You will also find tempo markings in English, such as "lively," "brightly," "somberly," "majestically" and so on. All of these terms leave a certain amount of interpretation up to you.

Variation on **Farruca**
Arr. Alan de Mause

In Flamenco music,* the rest stroke (sometimes called the "heavy thumb") strongly emphasizes the melodic bass notes. Notice how the fingers intermix with the thumb, and that the thumb sometimes plays the high strings.

Reminder: Notes with stems down are played with the thumb.

© Acorn Music Press, 1977

Note: V = upstroke; ⊓ = downstroke. Brush up and down across the strings in rhythm using your thumb.

*_Flamenco,_ the folk music and dance of the Spanish Gypsies, is played almost entirely on guitars. It is among the most exciting musical styles in the world. _Farruca_ is one of the many dance forms that make up Flamenco music.

Playing The Melody On The High Strings

Up to now you have been playing the melody in the bass notes, with chord or arpeggio accompaniment. Many of these pieces could have been played with a pick as well as with your fingers.

Can you play this with a pick?

You can see that when the bass and treble notes are separated this way, it is impossible to strike them together with a pick. Here finger-style playing is a necessity. Play it this way:

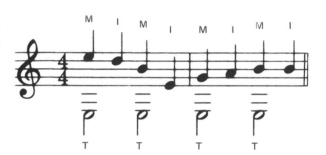

Pick the strings with your thumb and appropriate finger in a squeezing or pinching motion, your fingers moving towards each other in a relaxed free stroke. Alternate your middle and index fingers on the high strings. Here are some warm-up exercises for this technique:

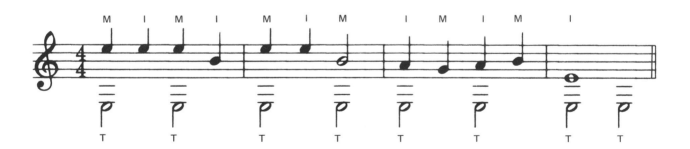

More movement in the bass:

Playing Notes In Harmony **(6ths)**

In the following exercise, the treble line is a C scale, and the bass line follows exactly six notes below it. Play both notes together, observing the left hand fingering carefully.

Spring Waltz

Simple Gifts

Shaker Song

'Tis the gift to be sim-ple, 'Tis the gift to be free, 'Tis the

gift to come down, Where we ought to be, And

when we find our-selves___ in the place just___ right, It will

be in the val-ley of love and de-light. When

true sim-pli-ci-ty is gained, To bow and to bend we will

not be a-shamed, To turn___ To turn___ will___ be___ our de-light,___ For in

turn - ing, Turn - ing we'll come___ 'round right.

Playing The G Scale In 6ths

Note that the B note in the second measure is fretted with the second finger on the 3rd string, fourth fret.

The First Noël
Christmas Carol

Amazing Grace
Southern Hymn

Treble Melody
And Accompaniment

In the following pieces the melody notes are in the treble (stems up), played primarily with the middle finger. The accompaniment (stems down) is played with the thumb and index finger. Notice how the melody is *ornamented* by the notes of the accompaniment weaving around it.

When you feel comfortable with this technique, strike the melody notes with a **rest stroke**. That is, come to rest on the next lower string. You will notice that this stroke produces a louder, sharper tone, just as it did in the bass. For this reason it is sometimes called an **accent** stroke.

Free Bird
Happy Traum

Eres Alta Y Delgada
(You Are Tall And Slender)
Spanish Folk Song

Playing In The Key Of A

The key of A has three sharps in its key signature, F#, C#, and G#.

Play the A scale, alternating index and middle fingers and using the rest stroke.

Dance
Anon.
Arr. Alan de Mause

Basic Chords In A

The basic chords in the key of A are A, D, and E7.

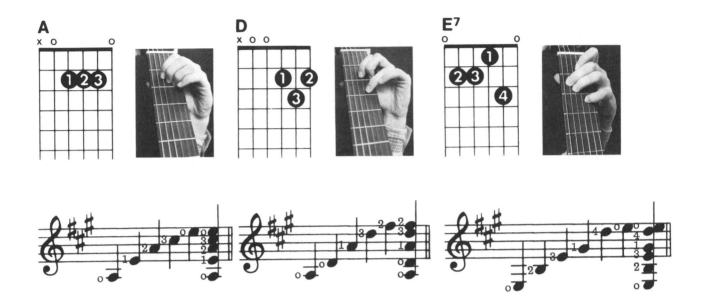

Arpeggio Study In A

Bass Run Study In A

Shenandoah

A wiggly line before a chord ⦚ tells you to "roll" the notes of the chord in a harp-like way. Start with your thumb, then I, M, R in a rapid movement, sounding each note in the chord separately.

31

My Grandfather's Clock

In this arrangement, the melody is sometimes in the bass and sometimes in the treble. It makes full use of the three octaves you know so far. Watch the fingering carefully.

Playing In The Key Of E

The key of E has four sharps in its key signature: F, C, G and D.

Play the following piece carefully. Don't forget the sharps!

Study In E

Basic Chords In E

The basic chords in the key of E are E, A, and B7. You already know the A and B7 chords. Here is E:

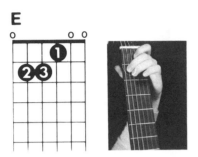

Arpeggio Study In E

Review

Write in the letter name next to the appropriate key signature.

Kumbaya

Blues In E

There are times that your thumb will play a rhythm chord to fill in a beat. Brush down across three strings in the places indicated.

Review

Write a harmony six notes below these scales as we did with the C and G scales. Then learn to play them.

Techniques And Touches:
Hammers, Slides And Pulls

Here are three widely used techniques which will add style and interest to your playing. Each changes the pitch of a string with the use of your *left* hand.

The **hammer-on** raises the pitch of a note. Pluck the string. While it is still vibrating, fret it hard enough so that it keeps ringing but sounds a new note.

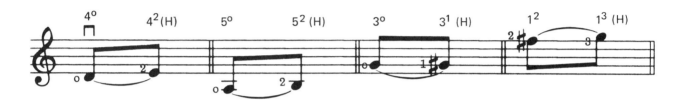

The **pull-off** lowers the pitch of a note. Play a fretted note. While it is still vibrating your fretting finger plucks the new note.

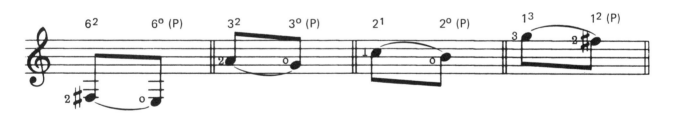

The **slide** can either raise or lower the pitch of a note. While pressing down the string at a given fret, pluck the note and while it is still vibrating slide your finger up or down the neck to the desired note. Maintain firm pressure or the second note will not sound.

In classical guitar literature, these techniques are called "slurs."

Etude With Hammers, Slides And Pulls

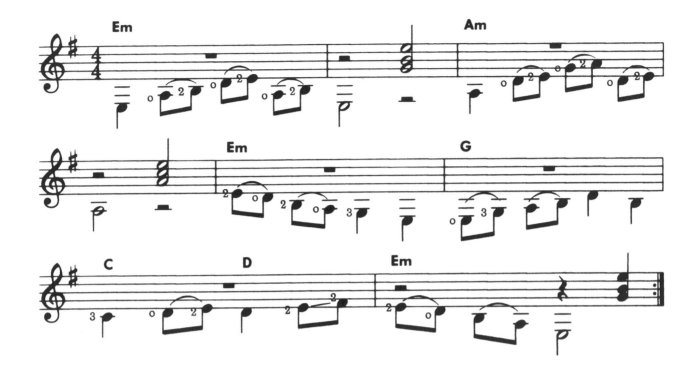

What You Gonna Call That Pretty Little Baby?
Spiritual

Blues In A

Note: Be sure to have both fingers in position before pulling off from one fretted note to another.

For example:

from **Gavotte**

J. S. Bach

Allegro moderato

Rhythm Session:
$\frac{12}{8}$ Time

Do you recall the specific meaning of the two numbers in a time signature? $\frac{4}{4}$

The top number tells you how many beats are in each measure. In this case, there are four beats to a measure.

The bottom number tells you what *kind* of note gets one beat. In this case, each beat equals a **quarter note**. How would you interpret this time signature? $\frac{12}{8}$

How many beats to a measure? What kind of note gets one count? Answer: There are twelve beats to each measure, and each count equals an eighth note.

Just as in $\frac{6}{8}$ time, the notes are counted in groups of three.

Example:

Because it gives a feeling of triplets, many blues and rock songs are written in $\frac{12}{8}$ time.

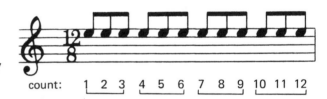

count: 1 2 3   4 5 6   7 8 9   10 11 12

Review

Write the time signatures for the following tune fragments.

40

Exercise In $\frac{12}{8}$

Rhythm Session:
Counting In $\frac{12}{8}$ Time

R & B Bass

A Tribute To Fats Domino

The following piece combines the *Exercise in* $\frac{12}{8}$ and the *R&B Bass* to create a two-part instrumental in the style of one of the great early rock/blues pianists.

Playing Folk-Style Fingerpicking

In folk-style fingerpicking, the thumb often maintains the rhythm with a steady bass pattern. Playing on the beat (every quarter note) the bass alternates between the **root** (the bass note with the same name as the chord you are playing) and another bass note within the chord.

In this type of playing, the thumb becomes your rhythm section, so it is essential that you develop a strong, steady sense of time.

In *The Bluebird* you will be playing a steady bass with the melody notes playing *on* the beat (with the bass).

The Bluebird

Now you will be playing both *on* the beat (at the same time as the thumb) and *off* the beat (between bass notes). The essence of this style is the **syncopation** that occurs between the bass and treble notes.

In the following piece, notice that the syncopated notes anticipate the beat. Sometimes you will find that a note will even be played in the measure before the chord actually changes.

John Henry

Learn to play these songs from memory.

Hard, Ain't It Hard

Moderately

Aunt Rhody Rag

Briskly

Graduation Recital

You have now learned the basics for several types of finger-style guitar. Here are three final songs which should be learned and memorized. Then you can play them for your family and friends.

Fingerpickin' Rag

Theme From Bourée

J. S. Bach

Moderato

Lute Piece From The Renaissance

Anon.
Arr. Alan de Mause

Andante

CONGRATULATIONS!

You have now completed Book 3 of Happy Traum's Basic Lessons, and you are ready to go on to Book 4.

In the next book we will continue to explore various guitar styles and techniques which will provide you with new and challenging pieces, strengthen your skills, and round out your basic guitar education in preparation for more advanced studies.

Play guitar with Happy Traum.

Basic Guitar Lessons.

Book Four.

To the Teacher

In Basic Guitar Lessons Books 1 and 2 we worked with pick style playing to acquaint the student with elementary technique and the elements of note-reading and understanding. Through many kinds of music from folk to classical, the student expanded his repertorie and, by the end of the second book, was able to play single notes and some chords in an accomplished and musical way.

Fingerstyle playing was introduced in the third book in order to expand the instrument's possibilities and further develop the talent of the student. Many more techniques and styles were made possible, and he learned a wide variety of new and interesting material.

This fourth volume of Basic Guitar Lessons brings together both pick and finger styles, reinforcing the techniques previously taught while introducing enough new material to serve as an introduction to the intermediate and advanced study he wishes.

It is my hope that with your help and guidance, your student will have acquired the tools he needs to feel that wonderful sense of accomplishment when he plays well for his teacher, family and friends. These books are only a beginning, but that is the most important part of any endeavor.

To the Student

Having reached the fourth book of Basic Guitar Lessons, you have learned quite a bit about the guitar and are able to play and sing in a variety of styles. Now, in this book, you will solidify your knowledge and technique, and prepare for more advanced study in the area that you and your teacher choose.

In Book 4, you will be playing both pick and finger style, as I feel it is important for the contemporary guitarist to be familiar with all of today's techniques. Versatility is the key to success, and a well-rounded knowledge of your instrument will open the door to many new musical experiences.

I hope that while learning the new material in this book you will also enjoy the music you are making. I have tried to provide musical examples that will be both interesting and stimulating. Learn them and play for your family and friends. The reaction from your listeners will surely spur you on to new avenues of musical exploration.

Good luck!
Happy Traum

© 1977 Acorn Music Press
Published © 1984 Amsco Publications
A Division of Music Sales Corporation, New York
All Rights Reserved

Exclusive Distributors
Music Sales Corporation
24 East 22nd Street, New York, NY 10010 USA
Music Sales Limited
78 Newman Street, London W1P 3LA England
Music Sales Pty. Limited
27 Clarendon Street, Artarmon, Sydney NSW 2064 Australia

International Standard Book Number: 0.8256.2359.6
Library of Congress Catalog Card Number: 75-32886

Printed in the United States of America by
G. Schirmer, Inc.
7/84

Amsco Publications
London/New York/Sydney

Review

You have learned many skills and techniques in the three previous books of Basic Guitar Lessons. Those reviewed below should help remind you of some of the more important ones and help you get started on Book 4.

In finger style playing, right hand fingering is notated as follows:

    T=thumb;   I=Index; M=middle; R=ring

Numbers next to a note indicate left hand fingering.

Unless otherwise indicated, notes with stems down are played with the thumb, stems up with the index, middle, or ring fingers.

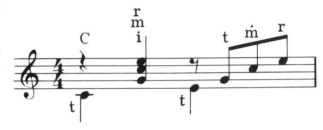

A 𝄾 before a chord tells you to "roll" the notes, starting with your thumb, then I, M, and R in a rapid movement giving a harp-like effect.

The **hammer-on** raises the pitch of a note by fretting the string with a finger of the left hand after it has already been plucked.

The **pull-off** lowers the pitch of a note by plucking it with the left hand.

Both techniques are indicated by a slur line.

In pick style playing, ⊓ tells you to pick in a downward direction. V tells you to pick in an upward direction.

It is important to be able to alternate between down and up strokes when playing notes in rapid succession.

Songs for Review

Welcome In! Duet

Pick Style

The Seeds of Love

Finger Style

Traditional

You should have no trouble playing the next song. The only new item is the use of the B minor chord. Bm is the relative minor in the key of D.

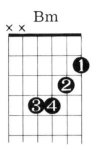

The Battle Hymn of the Republic

Two Bluegrass Songs

Rhythm Session:
Sixteenth Notes

An eighth note can be divided in half to make two sixteenth notes.

Four sixteenth notes equal one quarter note.

Be sure to play and count these sixteenth notes evenly.

One e and a two e and a three e and a four e and a

A sixteenth note rest looks like this:

Bluegrass is usually played "flatpick style." It is a good way to develop your technique.
Play with a steady rhythm, counting carefully.

Flop-Eared Mule

Pick Style

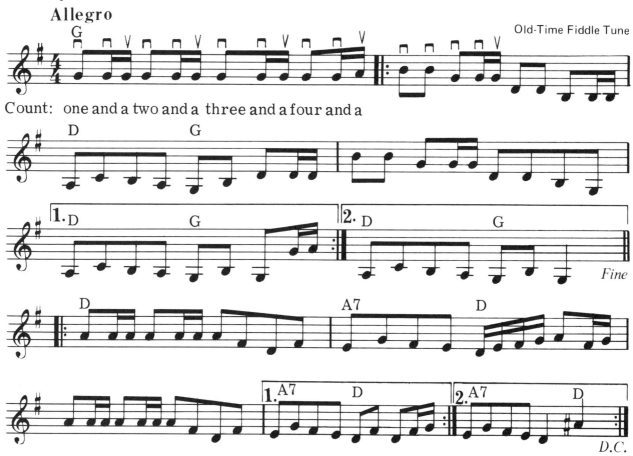

Count: one and a two and a three and a four and a

Golden Slippers

Pick Style

Allegro

Country Dance Tune

High B and C

By adding two notes: high B  and high C you can play the C scale in two octaves:

Play Evenly:
ascending scale

When played as a duet, the melody of *Wanderin'* (guitar 1) can be played pick style. The accompaniment (guitar 2) should be played finger style. As in the other duets in this book, the student should learn both parts.

Wanderin'

My Dad-dy is an en-gin-eer, my bro-ther drives a hack; My sis-ter takes in laun-dry while the ba - by balls the jack, and it looks like _____ I'm ne-ver gon-na cease my wan - - der - in'.

Traditional

This beautiful melody by J. S. Bach will give you excellent practice reading and playing eighth and sixteenth notes. Follow the fingering carefully. When you have learned it, play it for your family and friends.

Sleepers Wake!

Pick Style

J.S. Bach

8

Intervals

Chords and harmony notes are based on the concept of **intervals**, the distance between two notes. The smallest fretted interval on the guitar is a half-step. The major scale is made up of whole-step and half-step intervals in this order:

Reminder. The same note will often be described in two different ways, with either a sharp or flat name. For example, F♯ is played on the same fret as G♭. C♯ is played on the same fret as D♭, and so on. These notes are called **enharmonic**. Their name is based on the key or scale they are in.

The name of an interval is found by counting the number of half and whole steps between the two notes.

| Unison | Maj 2nd | Maj 3rd | Perfect 4th | Perfect 5th | Maj 6th | Maj 7th | Octave |

If you "flatten" the major intervals, making them a half-step smaller, they become minor intervals.

| Unison | Min 2nd | Min 3rd | Perfect 4th | Perfect 5th | Min 6th | Min 7th | Octave |

Work Sheet: Thirds

Some of these intervals are major thirds, while others are minor thirds. Find the name of each by counting in half-steps from the bottom note, and write the name of the interval.

Hint: A major third contains four half-steps, while a minor third contains three half-steps.

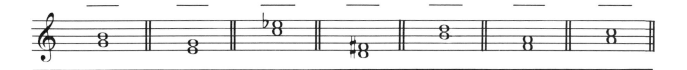

Playing Harmonized Scales

The following C scale is played in intervals of major and minor thirds.

It is often necessary to play notes in a different position from those you are used to. Until now, D has been played on the open 4th string. Since F♯ is also played on the 4th string, the D must now be played on the 5th string, fifth fret.

The B will sometimes be played on the 3rd string, fourth fret.

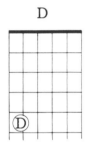

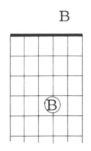

E can be played on the 2nd string, fifth fret.

When a different string from the usual is required, it will be indicated by a circled number.

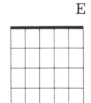

Etude in Thirds

All 'Round My Hat

Pick Style

English Folk Song

All 'round my hat I will wear a green wil - low. All 'round my hat for twelve months and a day, and if an - y - bod - y asks: me the rea - son why I wear it, it's all for my true love who's far far a - way;

Work Sheet:
Harmonizing Practice

Directions: Continue writing in the harmony notes (in thirds) and then play the song. Can you figure out the title of the song by listening to yourself playing it?

Finger Style

Words and Music by Jimmie Davis and Charles Mitchell

Harmonizing a Melody

We have spoken of the three basic chords in each of the keys we have studied. These chords are based on the first, fourth, and fifth notes of the scale that the song is in.

In the key of C, the basic chords are C, F, and G7.*

Write in the scales to find the basic chords in these keys:

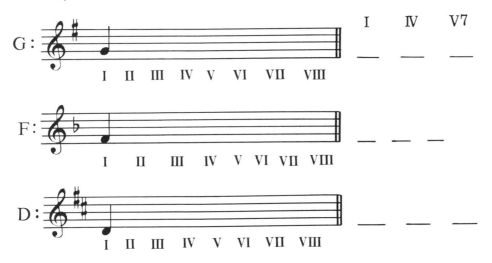

Many songs can be accompanied by only two chords, the I and V7. Write the chord accompaniment of these melodies.

*The chord based on the fifth tone of the scale (V) is usually played with an additional note, making it V7. This helps lead your ear back to the first (I) chord. The V7 chord is called the *dominant seventh*.

Harmonizing and Ear-Training

The following songs should be accompanied by the I, IV and V7 chords. Play the melody, listening for the correct harmonization. Then write in the chords and play them while someone else plays the tune. What song is this?

American Folk Song

Hint: Notice that **most** songs begin and end on the I chord. The V7 chord often leads back to the I.

Rhythm Session:
Dotted Eighth Notes

A dotted eighth note is equal to an eighth plus a sixteenth note.

A dotted eight plus a sixteenth equals a quarter note.

Count carefully. Try to get the **feel** of the dotted eighth and sixteenth note combinations.

One e and a two e and a three e and a four e and a

The following piece is in the key of A. Add the letter names of the accompaniment chords indicated by the roman numerals. Then play both the melody and the accompaniment.

The Johnson Boys

Pick Style

The dotted eighth-sixteenth note pattern is sometimes called the **shuffle rhythm**. It is often used with blues and rock songs.

E Train Shuffle

Pick Style

Reminder: This sign 𝄽 tells you to rest for the equivalent time of a sixteenth note.

In the piece below, the bass notes carry the melody. Play them with a rest stroke.

October Song

Finger Style

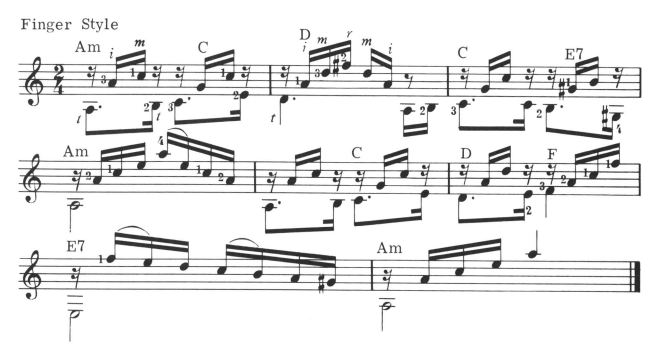

Playing F, F Sharp and G on the Second String

You already know that if you fret the 2nd string at the fifth fret you will be playing E (the same as the open 1st string). If the 2nd string is fretted at the sixth fret, you will have a new position for F (2^6). F♯ is one fret higher (2^7). To play G on the 2nd string, fret it at the eighth fret (2^8). Now you can play E, F, F♯, and G on the 1st *or* 2nd string.

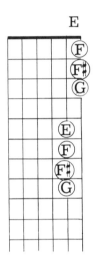

She Moved Through the Fair

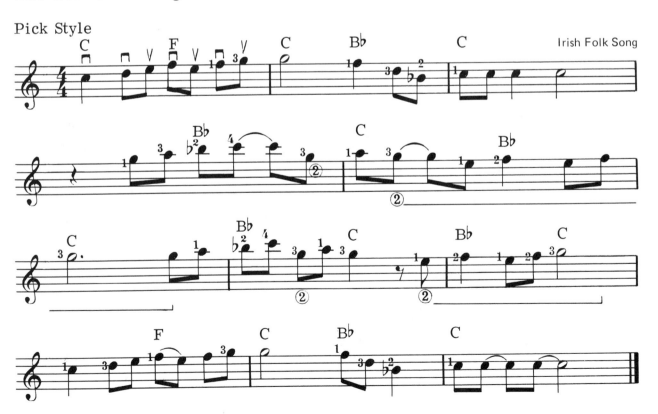

Pick Style   Irish Folk Song

16

Road To The Isles

Finger Style

Scottish Dance

The G Scale in Thirds

In this exercise, the A is played on the 6th string, fifth fret. Previously it was played on the open 5th string.

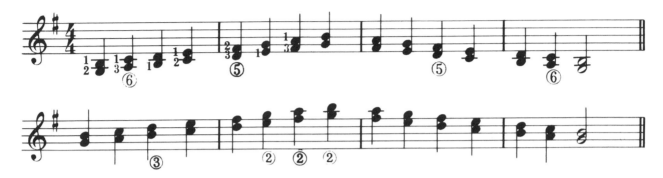

Play the following piece slowly at first. As you build up speed, be sure to keep the tempo even.

Coaster

Pick Style

Must I Leave? (Muss I Den?)

German Song
Arranged by Alan de Mause

Finger Style

Note: The symbol C in the time signature denotes **common time**, which is another way of saying $\frac{4}{4}$ time.

There are some unusual hand positions in the next song. Follow the fingering carefully.

La Perla

Finger Style

Spanish Folk Song

The next song illustrates the use of **unison** notes. In some places the G is played on two strings at once—the open 3rd string and the 4th string, fifth fret.

Au Clair De La Lune

Finger Style

French Song
Arranged by Alan de Mause

The G Scale In Tenths

When the harmony notes in thirds are played an octave higher, they are called **tenths**. This means that the harmony notes are ten notes away from the scale or melody.

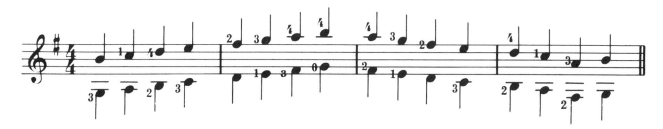

Kommt Ein Vogel Geflogen

Austrian Folk Song

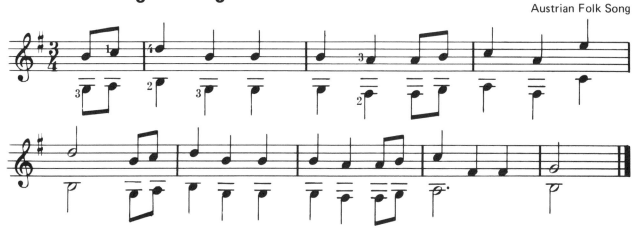

Joy To the World

Finger Style

G.F. Handel

Playing Folk-Style Picking Patterns

The patterns written below can be used to accompany a wide variety of folk-style songs. When you change chords, the bass notes change but the basic pattern remains the same.

Practice each one over and over until it flows smoothly. Keep the rhythm steady and even.

John Hardy

The following fingerpicking pattern has a bouncy, syncopated feel to it. Pay special attention to the thumb part (stems down) since this provides a steady bass beat to counterpoint the off-beat treble notes.

Practice this pattern until you can play it easily with different chords. Then try *Bully Of The Town*.

Pattern #2

Bully Of the Town

Here is still another fingerpicking pattern. Notice that the accent has shifted to a different beat. Can you tell which one?

Man of Constant Sorrow

I'll bid fare - well | | to Cal - i -

G7

forn - ia, | the place where | I

C | | Am

was born and | raised.

| Dm

Chord Building

Triads

A chord is made up of two or more intervals. The simplest chord is called a **triad**. It contains three notes.

The names **root**, **third**, and **fifth** are given to the three notes of the triad. The root is the note on which the chord is built.

Fifth
Third
Root

A major chord (triad) is composed of a major third and a perfect fifth.

A minor chord (triad) is composed of a minor third and a perfect fifth

The notes of a chord can be played in any order, or **inversion**. When you play a chord on the guitar, one or more of these notes may be repeated. Read and play the following chords. Notice the triads that make them up.

Work Sheet

The following chords are in their **root position**.
Write the name of the chord above it.

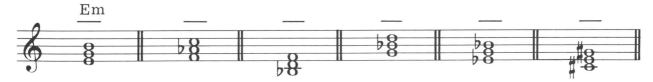

Now figure out and play the following chords. Write them below as you have played them on the guitar.

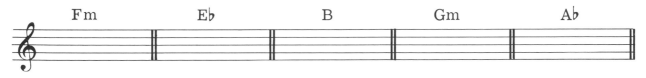

Sevenths

Adding certain notes to a chord can change its sound and character to make it more interesting or unusual. For instance, when we play a **dominant seventh** chord (G7, D7, A7 and so on), we are adding a minor seventh interval to the chord.

A more modern and jazz-like sound can be heard when we add a **major seventh** interval to the chord. Play the following:

If you add a minor seventh interval to a minor chord, you get a **minor seventh** chord.

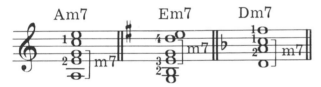

The following song illustrates the use of some of these chords. Your teacher or a friend can play the melody while you strum the accompaniment. Then switch parts.

Pick Style

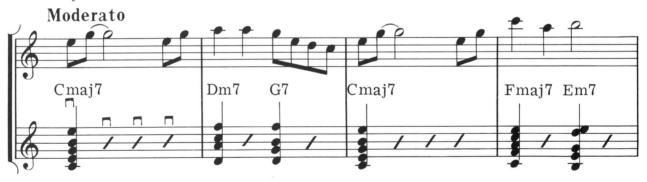

*These chords are usually played using the first finger as a *barre*.
 For a discussion of barred chords, see page 39.

Playing Movable Chords

If a chord does not contain any open strings, it can be moved to different positions on the neck of the guitar. The entire chord is raised by a half-step at each fret.

The Movable F

Play an F chord, strumming only the top four strings.

Move the entire chord up to the next fret. This is an F♯ or G♭ chord.

F♯ or G♭ (2nd fret)

When you play the F position on the third fret, you have a new way of playing G. Remember to strum only the first four strings.

G

Play the following exercise, moving smoothly from one chord to the next. When changing, do not lose contact with the strings. Relax your hand and slide from one fret to another.

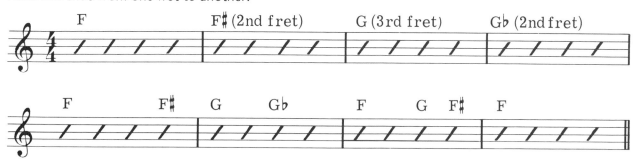

In this chord position, the chord takes its name from the note that is being played on the high E string. For instance, when you are playing the G chord, notice that you are playing a G on the 1st string, third fret.

This well-known Mexican dance tune has a distinctly Latin-American rhythm. Play the G chord in the F position on the third fret throughout.

La Bamba

Lead

Mexican Dance Tune

Playing Chords in the Key of B Minor

When accompanying songs which are in a minor key, the three basic chords are still built on the first, fourth and fifth notes of the scale (making I, IV and V chords). However, the I and IV chords are minor, while the V chord is often a major chord—the dominant seventh.

The basic chords in the key of B minor are Bm, Em, and F♯7. You already know Bm and Em. Here is F♯7:

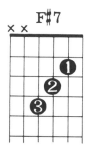

Theme From Etude in B minor

Fernando Sor

Stagolee

Lead

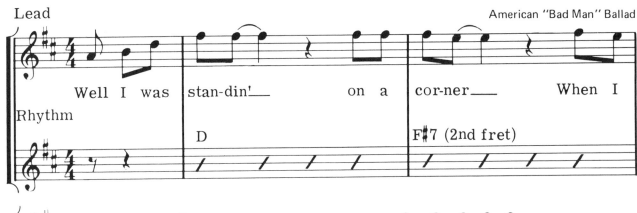

Well I was stan-din'___ on a cor-ner___ When I

Rhythm

D   F#7 (2nd fret)

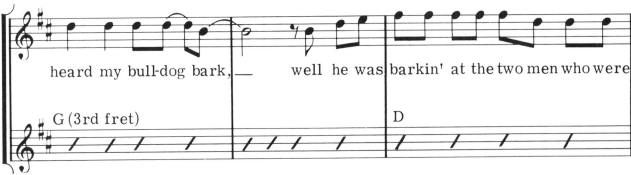

heard my bull-dog bark, ___ well he was barkin' at the two men who were

G (3rd fret)   D

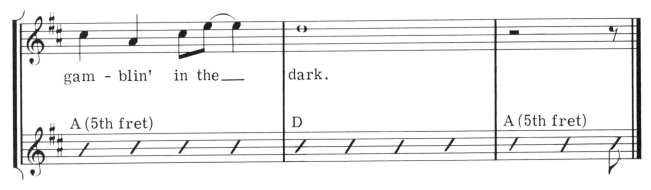

gam-blin' in the___ dark.

A (5th fret)   D   A (5th fret)

If you play the F position at the seventh fret, you will have a B chord.

B

Rockin' Rhythm

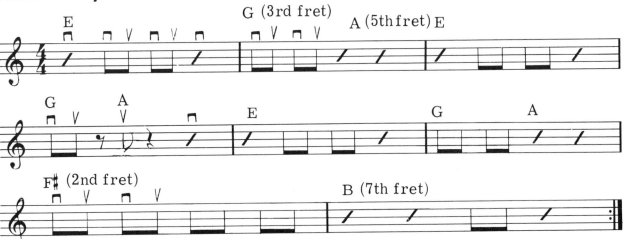

E   G (3rd fret)   A (5th fret) E

G   A   E   G   A

F# (2nd fret)   B (7th fret)

32

Playing Diminished Seventh Chords

Every diminished seventh chord can be named four ways, as it takes its name from each of the notes that make it up. Each diminished seventh chord is made up of three minor third intervals.

Here is how the 3 diminished seventh chords are played on the guitar:

E°,A#°, C#°, G°

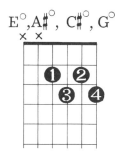

F°, B°, D°, G#°

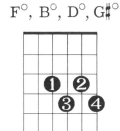

F#°,C°, D#°, A°

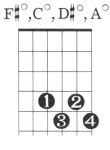

Since there are only 12 possible notes in the twelve-tone scale, a diminished seventh chord repeats itself every three frets. Play the diminished position at the first and second frets. Compare the notes you are playing with the diminished position at the fourth and fifth frets.

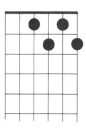

The notes in this chord are:
_____, _____, _____ , and _____ .

Play G°. Now find three other positions for the same chord. Find the G note in each position.

Note: Diminished seventh chords are symbolized in different ways. A G diminished, for example, may be written G°, G⁻, or G dim.

Combine picking patterns #2 and 3 (see page 23).

Make Me A Pallet On Your Floor

Lead

Traditional

Combine Picking
Patterns no. 2 and no. 3
(see page 22)

Make me a pal-let on your floor; make me a pal-let on your floor.

Make it soft, make it low so my good gal won't know Won't you make me a pal-let on your floor.

Gone Fishin'

Diminished Etude

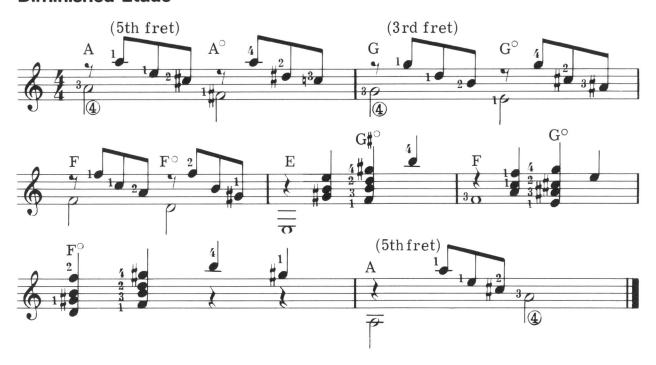

Review

Accidentals are sharps, flats, or natural signs not found in the key signature of the piece you are playing. An accidental is in effect throughout the measure in which it is written, but the bar line cancels it for the following measures.

Reminder: The sharp sign (♯) raises a note by one fret (a half-step).
The flat sign (♭) lowers a note by one fret (a half-step).
The natural sign (♮) cancels a previous sharp or flat.

Playing Accidentals

In the duet below, notice that you will be playing a C♭ note. This is played exactly the same as the more usual B note.

Jazz Duet

Pick Style
Guitar 1

Alan de Mause

Guitar 2

Follow the fingering carefully.

Double

J.S. Bach
Arranged by Alan de Mause

*$\frac{9}{8}$ is a new time signature for you, but it will not be difficult to play. Count nine eighth notes to each measure.

7th fret   6th fret

The Barre

The **barre** (or **bar**) is made by fretting two or more strings at the same fret with one finger, usually the index finger. You have already made a small barre when you played the F chord.

All of the barres you will study make movable chords, so they are very useful and important.

The 3-String Barre: F Minor Position

Notice that this position is very similar to the F chord. Only one note has been changed. Can you see which one? The minor chords that you will play in this position correspond at each fret to the major chords in the F position.

Hint: Keep your index finger flat and parallel to the frets. Press evenly and firmly across all three strings, exerting pressure from behind the neck of the guitar with your thumb.

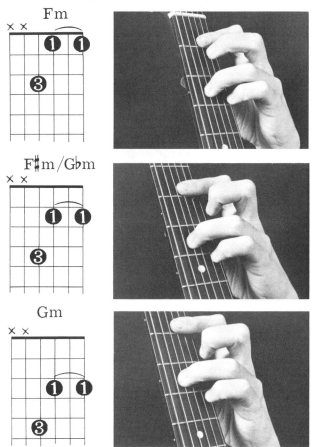

Fm

F♯m/G♭m

Gm

Quiz

Quiz: When you play the F minor position at the fifth fret, you get a _____ chord. At the seventh fret it is a _____ chord. At the fourth fret it will be a _____ chord.

Combining Movable F and F Minor Chord Positions

Red Clover

Hint: To move smoothly and quickly between these two movable chord positions, maintain a barre across the top three strings. You then need only to raise or lower your second finger to change between the major and minor forms of the chord.

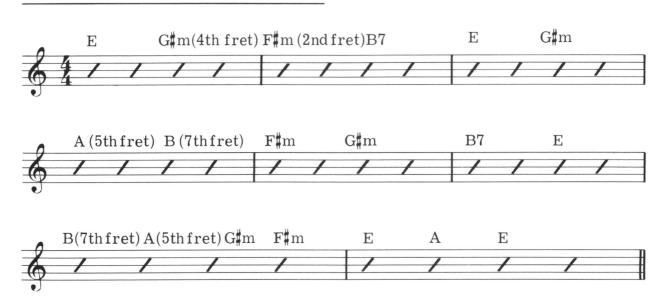

In classical guitar notation, the use of the barre is indicated by a roman numeral, which tells you at which fret your index finger makes the barre. If there is a 1/2 before the numeral, it means that you need to barre only three strings.

Andante

from Study No. 3

M. Carcassi

Chord Study:
Other Useful Movable Positions

The following three- and four-string barre chords will enable you to play a large number of chords in a variety of positions. They should be practiced and memorized.

Movable C Position

C#/Db   D   D#/Eb

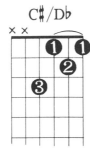 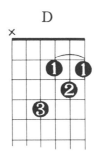 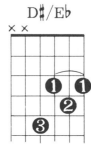

When this position is moved to the fifth fret it becomes a _____ chord. At the seventh fret it becomes a _____ chord. Play an F chord using the above chord position. Now play an A chord.

Movable A7 Position

A7   A#/Bb   B7

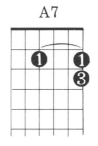 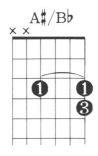 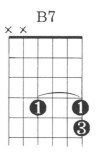

If you move this chord down one fret, it becomes a _____ chord. Move it up to the seventh fret. It is now a _____ chord. If you wanted to use this position to play a C7, you would move it to the _____ fret. For an Eb 7, you would move it to the _____ fret.

Movable F7 Position

F7   F#7   G7

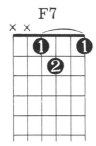 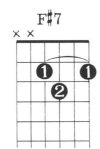 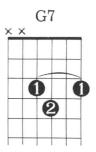

Using this position, play a B7 chord. Can you find two other ways to play B7? Can you find three ways to play A7? C7?

Techniques and Touches:
The Capo

A very useful tool for the guitarist, the **capo** is a small metal or elastic clamp that bars across all six strings simultaneously at any given fret. This raises the pitch of the entire guitar, a half-step each fret, enabling you to play open melody and chord positions in different keys. This is especially useful when the guitar is used to accompany the voice, since a familiar arrangement can be played in any key that the singer finds comfortable.

For example, if you place the capo on the third fret and play a song in the key of C, you will actually be playing in the key of E♭. If you know a piece in D but would rather play it in F, place the capo at the third fret and finger the notes as usual.

Capo Quiz

Place the capo across the fourth fret and play the chord positions for C, F, and G6. You are now playing in the key of ____ . The chords are ____ , ____ , and ____ .

Playing D, G, and A7 with your capo on the fifth fret, you are actually playing ____ , ____ , and ____ .

You want to sing in the key of F, but you only know the arrangement in C. Place the capo on the ____ fret.

A friend is playing his guitar in the key of G. You want to accompany him in a higher position. One possibility is playing in the D position with your capo at the ____ fret.

Fascination

Finger Style

F.D. Marchetti
Arranged by Alan de Mause

Graduation Recital

Buddy Bolden's Blues

Finger Style

New Orleans Ragtime

Blackberry Blossom

Pick Style
Lead **Allegro**

American Fiddle Tune

Rhythm

Invention No. 1 Duet

J.S. Bach
Arranged by Happy Traum

46

CONGRATULATIONS!

You have now completed Books 1 through 4 of Basic Guitar Lessons. If you have practiced and learned the pieces in these books carefully, you will have developed skills in many areas of guitar playing.

Where you take your achievements from here will be up to you and your teacher. There are many exciting guitar styles to pursue in a variety of musical fields. I have listed some publications below which should help you choose a direction.

I hope that these Basic Lessons have provided a firm foundation for whatever musical adventures lie ahead for you. Good luck!

Happy Traum

How to Play Blues Guitar
by Arlen Roth

How to Play Ragtime Guitar
by Christopher Camp

The Renaissance Guitar, The Baroque Guitar, The Classical Guitar
by Frederick Noad

Guitar Power
by Alan de Mause

A Folksinger's Guide to Flamenco Guitar
by Mariano Cordoba

Bluegrass Guitar
by Happy Traum

Contemporary Ragtime Guitar
by Stefan Grossman

The Country Blues Guitar
by Stefan Grossman

Delta Blues Guitar
by Stefan Grossman

Finger-Picking Styles for Guitar
by Happy Traum

Guitar Styles of Brownie McGhee
by Brownie McGhee and Happy Traum

Hawaiian Slack-Key Guitar
by Keola Beamer

Masters of Instrumental Blues Guitar
by Donald Garwood

Nashville Guitar
by Arlen Roth

Old-Time Country Guitar
by Fly Bredenberg and Stephen Cicchetti

Ragtime Blues Guitarists
by Stefan Grossman

Six Black Blues Guitarists
by Woody Mann

Traditional and Contemporary Guitar Finger-Picking Styles
by Happy Traum